FASHION

The 50 most influential fashion designers in the world

ISBN: 978 1 408 10631 0

Conceived and produced by
Elwin Street Limited
144 Liverpool Road
London N1 1LA
United Kingdom
www.elwinstreet.com

Jacket design: Diana Sullada
Picture credits: p. 23: 1935 Gabrielle Chanel photographed by Man Ray. © Man Ray Trust / ADAGP Paris 2009; Alamy: pp. 63, 74, 79, 87, 89, 117, 119, 120, 127; Corbis: pp. 9, 13, 29, 30, 33, 39, 45, 51, 54, 56, 61, 64, 69, 70, 73, 77, 82, 85, 87, 96, 99, 102, 107, 113, 123; Dreamstime: p. 90; Getty: pp. 10, 15, 17, 25, 35, 40, 42, 47, 48, 53, 59, 92, 95,105, 109, 111, 114; iStockphoto: p. 101; Kobal: pp. 37; The House of Lanvin: p. 21; Magnum Photos: p. 110; Prada SS09 collection: p. 81; Philip Treacy London p. 125.

The author would like to thank her research assistant, Ben Byrne.

A CIP catalogue record for this book is available from the British Library.

Printed in Singapore

FASHION

The 50 most influential fashion designers in the world

BONNIE ENGLISH

CONTENTS

Contemporary Avant-garde

Accessories / Leisurewear

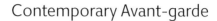

INTRODUCTION

The history of fashion is the history of its designers, each remembered best for the innovations or new styling that he or she has brought to the industry.

Who can think of Chanel without her No. 5 perfume, or Fortuny without his 'Delphos' gown or Givenchy without his 'Sack' dress? Mary Quant will always be associated with the miniskirt, just as Pierre Cardin will be with the 'maxi' and Hermès with scarves and handbags. Just as glamour is synonymous with Valentino, Balenciaga and James, casual lifestyle dressing is inherent in the designs of Armani and Lauren. How can we ever think of jeans without remembering Levi's, or men's underwear without thinking about Calvin Klein? Fantasy is synonymous with exotic Poiret, theatrical Galliano and Treacy's lavish hat creations, while tradition and longevity are the mainstays of Cartier jewellers, Karl Lagerfeld, and the House of Pucci.

Fashion has always been a product of its times and must be viewed within a broader cultural context. This context considers the designers' different ethnic and social backgrounds, changing social mores and attitudes, technological advances and the impact of economic and political events upon fashion trends. With a concise overview of the main ideas, innovations and key contributions of 50 of the world's leading fashion designers, this book makes the world of fashion accessible to everyone and provides a detailed and informative explanation as to why certain fashion trends emerged when they did.

The book considers four areas of fashion design: haute couture; prêt-à-porter; contemporary avant-garde; and accessories. Haute-couture (high-fashion) designers are considered the very best, governed in Paris by the Chambre Syndicale de la Couture, fashion's trade union, which determines who may be called an 'haute couturier'. There are currently only 18 official haute couture fashion houses in Paris. Prêt-à-porter or ready-to-wear designers mass-produce their fashion ranges instead of creating unique and exclusive 'one-off' models. Some designers produce both an haute couture line and a ready-to-wear line and, today, numerous designers offer a diffusion line – an associated brand of less expensive clothing.

Over the years, there have been many designers whose work defies classification. These are the ones who have pioneered new styling, techniques and ideas about fashion – in other words, they have broken traditions, smashed conventions and offered clothing that previously would not have been considered serious fashion apparel. These are the contemporary avant-garde designers.

Alongside these three main groups, and the designers of fashion accessories, the book explores ten fashion themes including the rise of the department store, fashion magazines, fashion photography, fabric technology, the emergence of the supermodel and the influence of street style on fashion. As such, this book offers a fascinating insight into the innovative world of fashion and its colourful designers – ideal for everyone with an interest in the subject.

Charles Frederick Worth

Charles Frederick Worth was an Englishman who, in the mid-nineteenth century, became the first arbiter of fashion in Paris. Worth's garments were displayed at the Great Exhibition of 1851, held at the Crystal Palace in London, England. Worth went on to open the first haute couture salon on rue de la Paix, Paris, in 1858.

Born 1825, Lincolnshire, England
Importance Established the rules and conventions of haute couture
Died 1895, Paris, France

The 'salon' had wide doorways and a spacious interior with a neutral colour scheme to avoid detracting from the colours of the voluminous skirts on view. Brilliantly lit chandeliers added elegance and luxury to the surroundings. Among Worth's clients were members of high society, royalty and foreign aristocracy. Celebrities, such as actors Sarah Bernhardt and Lilly Langtry, did much to publicise his beautiful gowns throughout Europe. As his reputation grew, Worth's gowns were sent overseas in huge steamer trunks to England, America and the colonies. Worth's name became synonymous with Paris fashion.

At the end of the nineteenth century, the period known as the Belle Epoque was characterised by excessive luxury and grandeur, and Paris fashions were considered too 'fast' for upper-class women outside France. Worth's gowns would often be left in storage for 5 to 10 years 'to age like port' before being worn in public (even then, they often were modified). Ironically, England's Queen Victoria was the only monarch at the turn of the century who did not wear Worth's dresses.

Worth's innovations were many: he shortened the daytime walking dress to the ankle in the summer of 1860; he created the 'Princess dress', which was cut in one piece rather than consisting of bodice and skirt; and he did away with the circular crinoline, introducing narrow skirts with a bustle back in 1899. The new 'diminished' fashion had a fair impact on the silk production at the Lyons factory and on the French textile industry in general.

During this period, a woman's extensive wardrobe included daytime clothing, usually made of 'serviceable' fabrics such as wool, linen or serge, and of conservative colours such as burgundy, navy blue, dusty pink or grey-green; while evening gowns were made of silk, moiré (watered silk), satin or tulle and more lightly coloured in pastel creams, pinks and lemons. Each garment was coordinated, in terms of colour and fabric, with hats, parasols, shoes, gloves and other accessories.

As the first couturier, Worth set standards by which other couturiers operated. He prepared his collection in advance and used live models (initially his wife) to present the clothes to an individual client in the luxury of his couturier salon. He would keep large rolls of beautiful fabric in his rooms so that his clients could choose from a wide selection. His sewing staff was sworn to secrecy so that each garment was entirely unique and custom-made to fit each client. A breach of this policy was met with immediate dismissal.

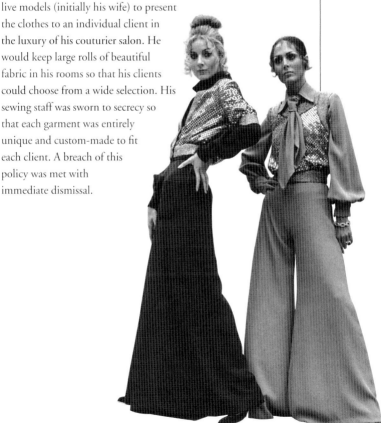

Madeleine Vionnet

Admired by her peers, renowned for the classic simplicity of her designs and heralded as the 'designers' designer', Madeleine Vionnet has left a legacy that few designers can claim. Just after the turn of the twentieth century, she worked for Callot Soeurs and then the House of Doucet, both in Paris. It was at the latter that she introduced her famous 'bias' cut, undoubtedly her greatest and lasting contribution to couture. She did not open her own, famous, couture house until 1922.

Born 1876, Chilleurs-aux-Bois, France
Importance Offered new methods of garment construction using fabric cut on the bias
Died 1975, Paris, France

Vionnet was a genius in the way she used materials and produced draped creations that were considered true works of art. Instead of drawing designs in the traditional two-dimensional manner, she preferred to use 36 cm (14 in) high mannequins – quarter-scale figurines – to manipulate and drape the fabric on the wooden forms. Influenced by Jacques Doucet, who was known for his youthful, free-flowing garments, Vionnet was instrumental in freeing women from wearing the corset and creating dresses that suited the 'modern' women of the early twentieth century.

Using a variety of 'cling' fabrics, such as crêpe de Chine, soft velvets and sleek satins, she experimented with variations of diagonally cut cloth. She encouraged textile mills to produce double-width fabric so that she could produce halter necks, cowl necks and dresses that needed no fastenings. While she was famous for her evening gowns, she also revolutionised lingerie so that it did not show any seams or gathers and appeared to float over the body as women's fashions, in particular, became looser and offered greater freedom of movement.

Vionnet showed her exotic garments, which looked like Grecian robes, without accessories and in equally unadorned salons. Her approach was very much a sculptural one: to dress a body, not to construct a dress. She preferred to dress tall, beautiful, well-proportioned women, as they best suited her superbly draped and timeless creations.

Vionnet's cutting techniques, which influenced many of the 1920s and 1930s designers, including Gilbert Adrian of Hollywood, had a huge impact on the creation of the slinky, body-hugging garments that became the trademark of 1930s films starring Jean Harlow and Gertrude Lawrence. They epitomised sensuousness and created a seductive appeal that suggested the contours of the body without revealing them. Edward Molyneux used these techniques to create the famous satin dresses that Lawrence wore in *Private Lives*, a classic Hollywood film.

It was argued that, owing to the complexity of their construction, Vionnet's garments were almost uncopiable and would have to be unpicked to reveal the secrets of her techniques. Despite this, however, she became particularly annoyed with 'copyists' and, in the 1930s, attempted to protect her designs from piracy by photographing the front, sides and back of a garment and registering her work with the Chambre Syndicale. She even went so far as to have her fingerprint included on the labels of garments that she exported to America in a bid to deter this fashion piracy. Vionnet refused to sell her designs to the trade as licensed designs and many felt that this led to her decline. She closed her salon in 1940.

> 'The dress must not hang on the body but follow its lines. It must accompany its wearer and when a woman smiles, the dress must smile with her.'

Haute Couture

HAUTE COUTURE AND THE CHAMBRE SYNDICALE DE LA COUTURE DE PARIS

Throughout history, one's social class has always been determined by the wealth and standing of one's family, and the wearing of fine clothing is an important determinant in marking your position in high society. During the second half of the nineteenth century, a new dictatorial hierarchy arose with the birth of 'haute couture', which literally means 'the finest needlework'.

Ironically, with the rise of the concept of the 'fashion designer' as distinct from the humble dressmaker, a new form of fashion elitism arose – one that was determined by wealth alone. Changing cultural values in society were reflected in the type of clientele frequenting Paris's 'high fashion' salons. Members of royalty and the aristocracy mingled with the 'nouveau riche' and celebrities of the stage. Haute couture designers offered individualised, made-to-measure garments using the finest fabrics that were decoratively embellished with a layering of lace, tulle and rich hand embroidery. The client chose the style, the fabric and the type of finishing she desired. The labour-intensive gowns required specialised hand-sewing techniques, and the workrooms were divided into bodice-making, skirt-making and sleeve-making areas, staffed by specialised sewers. Such high levels of craftsmanship and expertise contributed to the high prices of the resulting garments.

Paris became the centre of haute couture as, for centuries, France had been the leading manufacturer of beautiful fabrics, including silks, taffetas, velvets and brocade. By the 1920s, fashion became the fifth largest industry in France. In 1929 some of the leading haute couture salons introduced small ready-to-wear (prêt-à-porter) lines to counteract the copying of their more expensive couture ranges. A professional body, called the Chambre Syndicale de la Couture de Paris, was established in 1868, and was composed of haute couture houses and other firms that had made-to-measure dressmaking businesses in the Paris area. This union determined policy governing the fashion industry (such as copyright protection), established fair trading practices, organised major, biannual fashion collection showings on behalf of their members to facilitate the attendance of international buyers, and acted as a mediator between the press and the fashion industry. In 1873, it became part of the larger *Federation Française de la Couture, du Prêt-à-Porter des Couturiers et des Créateurs de Mode*.

During the Depression years of the 1930s it was necessary for the collection showings to be well organised, pre-publicised, and spaced over a 12 day period. The Syndicate negotiated with the textile manufacturers to supply fabrics to couturier houses on credit, with the accounts being paid after the collection was sold. Whilst most garments used larger amounts of material (as it was popular to use double-width fabrics), the number of garments paraded (usually around 100) were halved during this stringent time. The last coherent collection showing, before the outbreak of the Second World War, and the subsequent occupation of France by the Germans, was held in June 1940.

By the 1990s, the exclusivity of haute couture, as determined by the industry's powerful authority, the Chambre Syndicale, prevented many of the younger 'avant-garde' designers from joining the fold. This, coupled with a growing prêt-à-porter market that was attracting more of the wealthy young clientele, led to a decline in the number of haute couture salons. In the early 1990s, there were only 21 still operating in Paris; by the early 2000s this number had reduced to 11. Despite a loss of profits, many designers still show garments in haute couture collections as a way of creating publicity for their designer brands or diffusion lines.

Paul Poiret

Paul Poiret brought an oriental splendour to Parisian fashion with the introduction of harem trousers, pantaloons, wired lampshade tunics and hemlines weighted down by tassels.

Born 1879, Paris, France
Importance Freed women from the onstraints of the corset
Died 1944, Paris, France

Richly embroidered, glittering in brocade and swathed in fur, Poiret's brightly coloured garments with luxurious oriental themes brought an element of fantasy and exotica to haute couture that had never been seen before.

Poiret saw himself as an artist and a genius; he often dressed, somewhat pretentiously, in richly coloured cloaks and decorative turbans. His wife became his first model and his garments created an ideal of sophisticated luxury. While he begrudgingly acknowledged the genius of the costume designer Leon Bakst and his *Scheherazade* costumes for the Ballets Russes (1910), he insisted that his work was not directly inspired by this event.

As his garments were deliberately loose fitting, he contributed to the demise of the corset but preferred not to endorse this fact publicly, because it had such a detrimental effect on the undergarment trade in the first decade of the twentieth century. The Paris Chamber of Commerce sent a deputation to him in an attempt to dissuade him from pursuing this new 'unfettered' direction in fashion; among other things, it was considered to be immoral.

Poiret's considerable contributions to fashion included: being the first designer to introduce the 'V' neckline for daytime wear; bringing seraglio (silk screen-printing on fabric) into the salon; reflecting, in his collection, the violent primary colours of Bakst; introducing the 'hobble skirt' in 1911 and egg-shaped tunics in 1913; expanding his business to include interior furnishings (Martine School); and launching a series of exotic perfumes under the name '*La Parfumerie Rosine*'. An astute businessman, he was innovative in the marketing of his collection by commissioning top illustrators in Paris to produce a series of stylised drawings to promote his work. These artists included Paul Iribe (*Les Robes de Paul Poiret* 1908), Georges Lepape (*Les Choses de Poiret* 1911) and Pierre Fauconnet (*Fêtes de Bacchus* 1913).

In 1913, Poiret toured America with five of his models who paraded his garments in department-store fashion shows across the country. He successfully organised theatrical productions in the stores as well, in which the players wore his garments, thereby promoting his collection as a 'cultural' event. In order to establish a market in America, he designed a line of clothing that would appeal to American women, attaching a special label to these reproduction garments to identify their authenticity. Despite this, he found it was impossible to prevent unlawful copying of his garments as he, like others, became the victim of an extensive system of fashion piracy as New York became the international centre of ready-to-wear fashion manufacturing.

During these pre-war years, Poiret was the most celebrated dressmaker in Paris but his popularity waned after the war as his 'fancy dress' garments fell out of favour. He started to exhibit his work on barges which were tied to the Seine Bridge at the Paris International Exposition of Modern Industrial and Decorative Art, in 1925 and he continued to show his collection until 1929.

Jean Patou

The first designer to use his monogram as a design feature, Jean Patou worked in fashion from 1907 and established his couture house during the First World War. His clothing design was known for its originality and consistency in liberty, quality and prestige. Like Chanel (his legendary rival), in the 1920s, he realised that women wanted to be emancipated from Edwardian frippery and his collections included items such as sportswear, spectator clothes and beachwear.

Born 1887, Normandy, France
Importance One of the first couturiers to establish a ready-to-wear range
Died 1936, Paris, France

Patou was one of the first couturiers to recognise the need to develop a range of ready-to-wear clothes for his clients, which could be purchased in either small or medium sizes, with the price including one alteration. This marked a new direction in couture in 1929, and pre-empted the concept of 'designer wear' that we know today.

Patou's designs took their inspiration from prevailing artistic movements, including cubism and the strong, simple lines and geometric shapes of art deco. His clothes were also known for their beautiful embroidery, outstanding workmanship, hand-finishing and exquisite detailing. Significantly, during the 1930s, Patou became a pioneer of the modern machine-knitwear industry, creating cubist-inspired jumpers with matching hats, scarves and gloves, as well as the first knitted swimsuit. In 1932, he dropped the hemline and raised the waistline, reviving the *moyen-âge* silhouette that French *Vogue* magazine described as 'dreams of

'The modern woman leads an active life, and the creator must therefore dress her accordingly.'

beauty'. Chanel quickly followed suit and is, ironically, the designer credited with establishing the new silhouette.

Patou's shows were the event of Parisian haute society in the 1930s. As a precursor of today's obsession with dressing 'celebrities', Patou was famous for dressing tennis idol Suzanne Lenglen, Hollywood golden girl Mary Pickford and society notables Lady Diana Cooper, Louise Brooks and the Dolly sisters. Considered brilliant at public relations, and possibly the first designer to have invented the 'celebrity fashion show', he ensured that celebrities, journalists and friends packed the front rows of special preview parades for his couture lines, where he served champagne and gave out perfume samples.

Patou became renowned for his perfume ranges. He introduced 'Joy' in 1935, which continues to be popular to this day: it was named 'Scent of the Century' (UK's Fifi awards) in 2000, even outselling Chanel No. 5. In 1984, he re-released 12 commemorative fragrances: one of the revivals, 'Normandie', was created for the maiden voyage of the legendary ocean liner in 1935; another, '*Vacances*', originally commemorated the introduction of paid vacations in France in 1936; and '*L'Heure Attendue* (The Expected Time) was created in 1946 to mark the liberation of Paris two years earlier.

After his death, his brother-in-law Raymond Barkas took over the business. Other designers for the house have included Marc Bohan (1954 to 1956), Karl Lagerfeld (1960 to 1963; Jean Paul Gautier (1971 to 1973; Talazzi (1973 to 1977), Gonzales (1977 to 1982) and Christian Lacroix (1982 to 1987.

Mariano Fortuny

Inspired by a love of the oriental and a search for perfection, Mariano Fortuny revived ancient hand-pleating techniques to create his first pleated 'Delphos' gown in 1907. Crafted from the beautiful textiles he produced, the dress reflected a classical elegance that was reminiscent of ancient times. Patenting his methods for pleating and printing fabrics in 1909 and 1910 respectively, Fortuny became renowned for his unique garments of the utmost beauty.

Born 1871, Granada, Spain
Importance Revived an ancient form of classical design
Died 1949, Venice, Italy

Mariano Fortuny studied art and turned to textile design in the tradition of his father. In his Italian studio, he experimented with hand-printing metallic inks onto velvet and silk, to create the effect of brocades and tapestries. He first created 'Knossos' silk scarves in 1906, which were decorated with simple, geometric patterns and designed for dancers in the theatre to wrap around their bodies. Later that year, he extended his textile design into making garments, but ignored the constant stylistic changes dictated by the 'whims' of Paris fashion. Instead, he hand-pleated his garments using a very fine sheer silk in a manner similar to that used by the ancient Greeks. He finally opened a store in Paris, in 1912, and in New York City, in 1929, which sold his clothing lines and home furnishings.

His Delphos gowns were stored, wrung like skeins of wool, to keep the pleats intact. Each was made of four pieces of hand-mushroom-pleated silk, sewn together in a cylindrical shape, threaded through the neckline and sleeves with a drawstring and then weighted on the hemline with a line of Venetian iridescent-glass beads and tied at the waistline by thin silk cords. He made many variations of these 'un-corseted' gowns using different textiles often coupling them with unique velvet jackets and capes that were extremely loose fitting. They were hand-printed, first with woodblocks and, later, with a stencilled method using motifs that Fortuny copied from antique Byzantine, Italian and African textile designs and that gave the illusion of being brocades or tapestries.

He always maintained the tradition of haute couture, all of his work being entirely hand-sewn. His label, a circular piece of silk, hand-printed in gold metallic paint, was sewn to the lining of each garment. His techniques were labour-intensive and time-consuming, as every garment was an art form. Fortuny's knowledge of colour, as a painter, allowed him to overlay the dyes, which produced the most subtle tonal variations in the silk he used.

At the turn of the century, the Paris Exposition featured a new type of leisure garment, designed for wearing in the intimate surroundings of the home. These 'tea-gowns' (known as *négligées* in France) were endorsed by ladies of high society as they were seen as the ultimate luxury, and the most beautiful examples were designed by Fortuny and Madeleine Vionnet. It took 20 years for them to be worn in public as acceptable attire. Fortuny's work greatly inspired Paul Poiret who produced his own version of the Fortuny dress, and by the 1920s and 1930s, his gowns were growing ever more popular. The American designer Mary McFadden also revitalised a Fortuny dress in 1976 in honour of his outstandingly beautiful work and to highlight the timelessness of his classic creations. The ultimate simplicity and mastery of his work influenced many other contemporary designers, including Issey Miyake and Yohji Yamamoto. His work is held in all of the major museums around the world.

Jeanne Lanvin

Jeanne Lanvin started her own millinery business in 1890, introducing women's clothing in 1909 followed by menswear in 1926. After the birth of her daughter, Marie-Blanche, she

Born 1867, Brittany, France
Importance One of the leading couturiers to show her work at the Exhibition of Modern Industrial and Decorative Arts, in Paris, 1925
Died 1946, Paris, France

was inspired to custom-make children's clothing, which meant that the House of Lanvin was the only couturier designing for the entire family. Seeking reference from her extensive art collection (including works by Edouard Vuillard, Auguste Renoir and Odilion Redon) and a personal costume archive (consisting of garments from 1848 to 1925), her designs reflected her intensely personal, feminine preferences.

It was customary in the 1920s for a smart woman of social significance to be 'dressed', at no cost, by a couturier salon, provided that she was able to supply all the necessary accessories for the outfit, such as fur stoles and jewellery. Known as *mannequins de ville*, these women had a choice of 20 or 30 outfits to wear to special events of all kinds. Lanvin supplied such outfits for both a mother and her daughters, a form of promotion that proved to be very advantageous for business.

Lanvin's first success was the 'chemise' dress, fashioned before the war. Her next great innovation was the '*robe de style*', an adaptation of an eighteenth-century pannier. Introduced in the 1920s, it was reproduced in a variety of fabrics: silk taffeta, velvet and metallic lace with organdie chiffon and net. The garment was immortalised in 1922, when the illustrator, Paul Iribe, sketched Madame Lanvin and Marie-Blanche each wearing a *robe de style*. The image has been used ever since as the house signature on its labels and perfume bottles. The House of Lanvin released a number of fragrances, including, 'My

Sin' (1925) and 'Arpege' (1927 and re-introduced in 1994), a favourite of Rita Hayworth's and Princess Diana's, and still very popular to this day.

Lanvin became legendary for her colour sense; her famous 'Lanvin blue' was originally derived from the medieval blue stained glass seen in church windows. Decoration and patterning on her fabrics – in embroidery, appliqué and beading – became a defining characteristic of her work and she established three ateliers specifically for this purpose. She imported luxurious materials from the East and often lined her exquisite evening wraps with brightly-coloured velvets or satins. Other classic pieces included dinner pyjamas, hooded capes and zouave skirts.

Lanvin's illustrious clientele included the Princesses of England, the Queens of Italy and Romania, Mary Pickford, Marlene Dietrich, Yvonne Printemps and the poet Anna de Noailles. Being primarily an haute couture designer, her fashion house did not launch ready-to-wear collections until 1982 and the couture line was discontinued in 1992. Today, the current house designer for womenswear is Alber Elbaz with Lucas Ossendrijver taking over design of the men's line for the Spring 2007 collection.

Gabrielle (Coco) Chanel

One of the most famous designers of all time, Gabrielle Chanel's philosophy towards prét-à-porter undermined the need for exclusivity and uniqueness in fashion. Taking inspiration from men's clothing – particularly that of the military and working-class attire – Chanel created simple, practical clothes for a new generation of women who were active, held jobs and sought comfortable clothes.

Born 1883, Saumur, France
Importance Democratised fashion by bringing comfort and practicality to haute couture dress
Died 1971, Paris, France

Chanel's contributions to the evolution of fashion are numerous. One of her major innovations was her creation of the *pauvreté-de-luxe* look, where she combined fabrics such as jersey (used only for men's underwear) with elegant trims and buttons. She gave women's clothes masculinity by introducing garments such as sailor's trousers, jackets and sweaters. She emancipated women's dress through comfort and practicality and created a 'total look' that included accessories such as ropes of pearls, chain belts, two-tone shoes and the quilted bag with a shoulder strap nicknamed the 2.55 after the date it was created, February 1955.

Chanel immortalised the three-piece suit with pockets and flared skirts; she introduced imitation costume jewellery for daytime wear; in the midst of the Great Depression, in 1932, she also created her first range of fine jewellery, 'Les Bijoux de Diamants', made of platina and diamonds; and she made both short hair and a suntan fashionable. Above all, Chanel promoted a casual look for a time when women no longer felt it necessary to wear tight, uncomfortable clothes to impress.

Chanel's fashion garments of the 1920s were indicative of the 'machine-age aesthetic' that dominated design, and were characterised by standardisation, modularity and a streamlined silhouette. She used neutral colours, such as beige (her trademark), black, white and navy and fabrics such as jersey, velveteen, flannel, tweed, cotton and corduroy. Her greatest claim to fame was the 'little black cocktail dress', which she created in 1926. It was greeted by American *Vogue* as 'the frock that all the world will wear' and compared to the Ford T in allusion to its parallels with the vehicle's modernity and sobriety, which always come in black. Traditionally, black was reserved for mourning or the clergy – Chanel made it fashionable. It became so popular that it was called a 'uniform', worn by women around the world.

In 1927, once Chanel had persuaded the Scottish tweed mills to produce their fabrics in lighter pastel shades, she opened a shop in London to sell her tweed cardigan suits. These became popular for leisurewear as well as corporate wear, owing to their masculine appearance, which offered greater social mobility. At the same time, Chanel designed some of the most beautiful strapless evening gowns of the 1930s. Her versatility towards design ensured her professional and financial success, as she was able to respond to market demands. During the Second World War, the sales of her perfume, Chanel No. 5, soared as American soldiers returned from overseas with bottles for their loved ones. Today it is still a top-selling brand, with a bottle selling every 30 seconds.

Elsa Schiaparelli

Elsa Schiaparelli allied fashion with art and popular culture, introducing a levity not seen before in high fashion. In doing so, she did more than any other designer to break down the 'exclusivity' of haute couture fashion. She collaborated widely with artists, producing textiles and garments with surrealist artist Salvador Dali, among others. Renowned for her unusual and novel buttons, hats and embroidery, Schiaparelli was the first couturier to use zip fasteners on the pockets of a beach jacket, in 1930, and in a skirt in 1934.

Born Rome, Italy, 1890
Importance Combined fashion with surrealist art
Died Paris, France, 1973

Stylistically, Schiaparelli's clothing reinforced the silhouette of the 1930s, where slim lines replaced the loose, low waists of the 1920s, bodices became shorter and skirts were lengthened to mid calf. She gave women disciplined clothes with tight skirts under fitted waisted jackets, all immaculately tailored. She exaggerated broad shoulders by padding them or using sprays of coq feathers, elaborate embroidery or soutache braid for emphasis. These 'stressed' shoulders became the main feature of the 1930s look.

Although the evening dress with matching jacket was, perhaps, the greatest success of her career, it was Schiaparelli's hand-knitted sweaters with *trompe l'oeil* imagery that first attracted the attention of the fashion press. She commissioned an Armenian knitter to create a realistic 'bow' on the front of a garment, a trick that caught the attention of the editor of Paris *Vogue*.

Schiaparelli's designs highlighted her background as an artist, rather than a dressmaker – she had no couture training and she surrounded herself with painters, writers, poets and film-makers. She bolstered the button industry by requesting buttons of clowns, horses, acrobats, coffee beans and hand mirrors from the manufacturers. Her hats resembled high-heeled shoes, poached eggs and frilled lamb cutlets. She decorated her garments using zany, unconventional motifs printed and beaded onto fabric, and tirelessly pursued original fastenings such as zips.

'Women dress alike all over the world: they dress to be annoying to other women.'

The huge impact of surrealist art upon Schiaparelli's fashions was most evident in the year of 1938. In collaboration with Dali, she created the 'Tear' dress, where the fabric was printed with simulated rips and tears, creating a visual paradox of poverty and luxury, very much in keeping with notions of surrealism. She marketed a perfume called 'Shocking' in a bottle that represented the curvaceous silhouette of film star, Mae West.

In every aspect of her work Schiaparelli broke down the conventions of haute couture and replaced the seriousness of the industry with wit and humour. This offended many of the other designers of the day. Paul Poiret suggested that she contributed directly to the demise of haute couture and her arch-rival, Chanel referred to her 'as the Italian who made clothes'. Schiaparelli's work has influenced many contemporary artists and designers including Karl Lagerfeld, John Galliano and Alexander McQueen. She is one of the few fashion designers from the early twentieth century who directly consolidated the links between fashion and the fine arts. Fashion as art is a theme that has since been embraced by numerous curators and museum directors alike, and has been highlighted in major fashion exhibitions over the past 30 years.

THE RISE OF THE DEPARTMENT STORE

Most major department stores grew out of general stores, drapery shops or fancy goods stores. By the second half of the nineteenth century, companies wanting to promote their success in business commercially commissioned leading architects to design and build 'flagship' stores in major cities.

These department stores sold a diverse array of merchandise in one location and this convenience, in itself, ensured great financial returns. Stores such as Le Bon Marché in Paris, Selfridges in London, Macy's in New York and Isetan in Tokyo became household names. Marshall Field's in Chicago, which was designed by Henry Hobson Richardson, was deemed an architectural landmark, as it featured a large and magnificent Tiffany ceiling made of iridescent glass mosaic pieces.

In the nineteenth century, department stores included restaurants, restrooms or exhibition spaces, becoming social, as well as mercantile, centres. While they targeted mainly middle-class consumers, they also attracted the upper classes, owing to the opulence of interior design, which gave the illusion of aristocratic life. Methods of display became more seductive, more appealing in order to entice the customers to buy. Large display cases were used to house garments from the latest fashion collections. The displays became more elaborate presentations, generating great interest amongst artists, photographers and designers. When department stores introduced large, double-glazed windows at street level, which, after 1907, could be lit with electric light bulbs, the era of window shopping began.

Le Bon Marché, one of the oldest and most influential *grand magazins* in Paris set the benchmarks that led the way to the modern development of mass merchandising. The store sold cheaper, often mass-produced, goods with a guarantee of quality (normally only given to more expensive merchandise), introduced fixed prices – thereby doing away with bargaining – and offered customers the opportunity to inspect the goods without an obligation to buy and, if dissatisfied with their purchases, they could return the goods and receive a full refund. Le Bon Marché also sent out mail order catalogues, held special 'sales' and dramatically increased publicity and advertising. The commercial success of the French store was duplicated internationally and many existing stores, such as Selfridges on London's Oxford Street, were refurbished to attract a wider clientele (1907).

In the pre-First World War years, department stores began to hold fashion exhibitions, parades and theatrical events, which allied fashion, particularly haute couture, with culture. This occurred initially in America which, at the time, did not have exclusive couture salons, and so European couture fashions were paraded in both department stores and hotels, increasing the establishments' prestige and popularity. Having fashion parades and specialty designer spaces on the fashion floors of the large stores became a standardised practice during the period between the wars.

In the 1950s, department store credit cards and lay-by policies (paying a deposit) helped to increase sales, and other features such as air-conditioning, soft music and broader merchandising kept the stores financially buoyant. During the early 1980s recession, the stores found it more difficult to sustain customers, who were beginning to look for more personalised service and unique products. This corresponded to the rise of the 'boutique' trade.

Edward Molyneux

Edward Molyneux photographed his gowns in sumptuous surroundings – the interiors of well-appointed homes or draped over luxurious motor cars – and, during the 1930s, he became identified as the designer who epitomised the look. Simplicity and style prevailed in his designs, and brought an Englishman's sense of propriety and restraint to the pomp and pageantry of Paris fashion.

Born 1891, London, England
Importance Married restraint with perfect taste in dress
Died 1974, Monte Carlo, Monaco

Molyneux was the master of understated elegance. His clothes reflected a sense of perfect taste, and fashion journalists found it very difficult to write about his showings, as there was nothing showy, exaggerated or unconventional. He designed for royalty, Hollywood, theatre and films, becoming famous for the clothing he designed for Noel Coward's classic play, *Private Lives*, in which Gertrude Lawrence wore white wide-trousered lounging pyjamas, suits with fur collars and cuffs, and bias-cut evening dresses. He was well-known for his lingerie, hats and perfumes, and his delight in the use of furs. He rarely used drapery and preferred the look of modern sophistication. One garment that brought him particular fame was a white satin evening dress of streamlined elegance, which became the silhouette of the 1930s female figure.

Molyneux was first employed at the House of Lucile as a sketch artist and later as a designer at the Paris branch. At the time, the 'house styling' was very ornate and extravagant, heavily inspired by oriental influences, such as elaborate appliqué and ostrich feathers. When he completed his service during the First World War, he opened his salon in Paris, which he decorated in shades of grey with chandeliers and Louis XIV furniture. His assistants wore grey crêpe de Chine dresses.

The colour scheme that he preferred for his collections centred on black, grey and white, despite the usual bright colours that characterised the decade. A Molyneux ensemble differed from one by Chanel or Vionnet in its rejection of the intricate details of dressmaking: he preferred the simple style of lapel, collar and cuffs; all functional or structural details were discreetly hidden. His clients knew that they would always be dressed comfortably, in the best of taste and fashion, for any occasion. In 1937, his evening gowns were considered the most romantic in Paris. Due to the universal appeal of his designs, his clothing became staple items in every fashionable woman's wardrobe.

During the Second World War, Molyneux returned to Britain where he chaired the Incorporated London Fashion Designers' Society, designing prototypes for mass-produced clothing (Utility clothing). While items were simple and functional, the clothing was extremely well-designed and offered, perhaps, the only affordable opportunity for working-class people to wear well-constructed fashion goods. When Molyneux returned to his Paris salon, he found that it had been bombed during the war and very few of his designs survived. He lost heart trying to re-establish himself and finally closed the salon doors in 1950. Fifteen years later he attempted to establish an affordable ready-to-wear operation with his nephew, John Tullis, called Studio Molyneux, meant to cater for both French and American markets, but this venture was unsuccessful.

Charles James

Although born in England, Charles James is considered one of America's greatest couturiers. Photographer Cecil Beaton's iconic image of 1948, which shows a group of mannequins wearing dramatic James' evening gowns in the elegantly panelled room of a London residence, epitomises his contribution to post-war glamour. His clothes are known for their astounding complexity, beauty and use of luxurious fabrics.

Born 1906, Sandhurst, England
Importance Created clothes of great complexity and sculptural beauty
Died 1978, New York, USA

Bestowed with an obsessive personality, James was a perfectionist who was known to reconsider the construction and cut of a dress – even a single sleeve – for years. His output was limited as a result, but this was of no consequence, because he was uninterested in the cycles of fashion. However, his perfectionist drive and methods towards fashion did prevent him from entering the ready-to-wear market.

The complexity of the cut of his clothes produced garments that changed dramatically in appearance when looked at from different angles. Caroline Rennolds Milbank notes in her book, *Couture*, that James was 'always refining, always working towards a moment when it would exactly embody his vision. His evening dresses especially look as if they were captured in the moment of unfurling… they capture the essences of movement, they were "moments in time".' Undoubtedly, the sculptural cut of his clothes found its genesis in his training as an architect in

'Charles James is not only the greatest American couturier, but the world's best and only dressmaker who has raised the applied art form to a pure art form.'

Cristóbal Balenciaga

Chicago. His most famous ball gown was the 'Clover', based on the shape of a four-leafed clover. It was designed to be seen at best advantage from above, and consisted of four black velvet panels set into white satin. James always considered his dresses to be works of art and renewed and reworked similar designs over and over again.

Often made from vast quantities of fabric (up to 25 metres/27 yards), using luxurious materials such as satin, velvet and tulle, and underlaid with three differently cut petticoats, they could weigh up to 7 kg (15 lb). Despite this, owing to James's mastery in distributing the weight of the fabrics, the dresses were reputedly as light as a feather to wear. He had a brilliant sense of colour and juxtaposed the most beautiful coloured linings with the more subdued colours of his jackets and coats, which included celadon sky blue, chestnut and various shades of rose.

James started as a milliner in Chicago, in 1926, and opened his couture house in London in 1930. Following bankruptcy, and with the outbreak of the war, he returned to New York, opening another couture house in 1940. His businesses fell in and out of bankruptcy for the rest of his life.

Christian Dior

Christian Dior's beautiful, ultra-feminine 'New Look' followed the pragmatic, masculinised style that had dominated the war years. He cleverly assessed the psychological mood of this post-war period, and his 1947 collection epitomised elegance, glamour and sophistication; women around the world embraced the hourglass silhouette once more.

Born 1905, Normandy, France
Importance Reinstated the post-war feminine silhouette
Died 1957, Tuscany, Italy

Dior apprenticed with Piguet, Lelong and Balmain before opening his own salon in 1945. His design career was cut short when, after 13 years, he died suddenly, leaving a legacy with which few others could compete. His sculptural creations, like those of Cristóbal Balenciaga, were fashioned using firm, synthetic materials including stiffened nylon, rayon and composite fabrics, which were 'heat set' to hold their shape. He contended that shape guided him first, then fabric, then colour. His work was characterised by a use of elaborate construction techniques that had historical precedents in the nineteenth-century Victorian and Edwardian eras. These included built-in petticoats and mini-waisted corsets, hip padding, bodice and skirt lining, reinforcements of seams and pleats, and the weighting of jacket and skirt hems. He said, 'Without foundations, there can be no fashions'.

Dior reinstated the feminine silhouette after the style of the war years which had been influenced by the rations on fabric. Small waists, off the shoulder necklines and billowing skirts captured the hearts of the fashionable elite and Dior reinstated Paris as the centre of haute couture. From an economic point of view, it was crucial for France to retain her position, not only to support fashion, but the textile industry as well. For his achievements, Dior was awarded the prestigious *Médaille d'Honneur* by the French government.

Dior's evening gowns often used exorbitant quantities of fabric, ranging from 15 to 80 metres (50 to 260 feet). His elegant, strapless gowns had boned corsets built into closely fitted bodices. In the late 1950s, Dior introduced very stylised silhouettes, which he called his A line and H line (1955), Y line (1956) and Freeline (1957). By this time, with international sales of couture, prêt-à-porter, hats, shoes, furs and perfumes, his fashion empire earned the description, 'General Motors of Haute Couture' in the *New York Times*. His New York branch alone employed 1,200 people spread over 28 workrooms and included a private police force to prevent pirating.

When Dior died, his apprentice, Yves St Laurent became the head designer and continued the long era of loose shapes, clearly evident in his first Dior collection called the 'Trapeze' line of 1958. These unwaisted garments, which hung from the shoulders, opened couture to the larger figure and 'mothers-in-waiting'. The Dior label now trades under the Moët Hennessy-Louis Vuitton (LVMH) syndicate and John Galliano has been its recent head designer. Galliano has managed to recreate the image of quality, exclusivity and good taste.

Cristóbal Balenciaga

Dubbed the 'couturiers' couturier', Cristóbal Balenciaga was one of the most highly respected haute couture designers of all time. A prolific designer, whose career spanned a period of over 35 years, he is credited with creating every major fashion silhouette during that time. His fashions appeared regularly on the front pages of *Vogue* and *Harper's Bazaar* magazines.

Born 1895, Guetaria, Spain
Importance Epitomised the ultimate in elegance, grace and luxury
Died 1972, Valencia, Spain

Having trained as a tailor in San Sebastian, Spain, Balenciaga was able to apply his skill in creating simple, elegant and sophisticated forms. His greatest talent was an ability to mould garments into sculptural shapes. He also elaborately beaded or embroidered the surface of his fabrics, so that the sumptuous fabrics were highlighted by magnificent surface textures, an art that welcomed revival following the depression years.

Balenciaga opened his Paris salon on Avenue George V in August, 1937, just prior to the outbreak of the Second World War. It is, perhaps, for this reason that he is better known for his late 1940s and 1950s work. His clientele included the rich and famous, as well as members of royalty. Among them were Pauline de Rothschild, Mona von Bismarck and Jackie Kennedy. His favourite models were 'Colette' and 'Bettina', middle-aged brunettes whose figures and colouring were similar to those of his best clients. Balenciaga's astute business acumen and his genius for exquisite design ensured a very successful couturier career.

He chose fabrics that were naturally stiff, such as taffeta, velvet and layers of organdie, as they held their shape and complemented the defined forms of his garments, including his famous black 'Pumpkin' or 'Balloon' dress of 1950, his white organdie 'Flamenco' dress and his black and white 'Fishtail' dress, both designed in 1951. While the dominant colour for evening wear in the 1950s was black, daytime colours included brownish-red, yellow ochre, turquoise blue and mauve – the colours of his native homeland, Spain. It is significant that they also became the signature colours of the 1950s fashion period, and indicative of the influence that he had over fashion at that time.

Balenciaga's clothing often referenced both historical and non-European cultural garments, drawing upon past fashion styles. Inspirations included the sixteenth-century farthingale skirts seen in paintings by the Spanish master Diego Velasquez and eighteenth-century flowing coats depicted by the French rococo painter Jean-Antoine Watteau. In the early 1950s, Balenciaga's work reflected an oriental influence with mounted collars and three-quarter 'kimono' sleeves. He transformed the silhouette by broadening the shoulders and letting out the seams, thereby removing the waist, making this 'semi-fit' styling very fashionable. These loose, unfitted garments became, by 1957, the prototype for the kite-shaped 'sack' dresses made famous by his disciple, Hubert de Givenchy.

Expertly constructed, lavish and profoundly romantic, Balenciaga's clothing characterises the best of haute couture. His work is now part of the collection of every major art museum in the world and his fashion house, following his retirement in 1968, became part of the Gucci group with Nicolas Ghesquière appointed as head designer.

Hubert de Givenchy

Hubert de Givenchy became well-known for reviving an elegant and structured evening wear that was typical of the traditional couture houses. His clothes are best known for their simple and refined elegance, exemplified by his signature white cotton shirting (variations of which appeared in every collection). He is also recognised for the iconic 'little black dress' he designed for his great friend and muse, Audrey Hepburn, in *Breakfast at Tiffany's*.

Born 1927, Beauvais, France
Importance Revived the elegance and sophistication of traditional haute couture

Givenchy worked with Jacques Fath, Robert Piguet, Lucien Leong and Elsa Schiaparelli before establishing his own couture house in 1952, at the age of 25. During the 1950s, silhouettes became more defined and shapes such as the A line, H line and Y line, initiated by Christian Dior determined the direction of fashion styling. Greatly influenced by his close friend Cristóbal Balenciaga, Givenchy not only studied Balenciaga's garments and sketches carefully, but attended his actual fittings as well.

When both Dior and Balenciaga widened the silhouette by letting out the seams in the late 1950s, they created a 'freeline' look – a style that was embraced by full-figured women as well as mothers-to-be. Givenchy, in response, designed the 'Bubble' dress in 1956, which was subsequently featured in the Barbie doll wardrobe (1959) and the triangular loose-fitting garment, which hung from the shoulders and became known infamously as the 'Sack' dress. When *Time* magazine included photographs of the new chemise look, the underlying caption asked what had happened to the female shape. Givenchy replied that the Sack dress 'was inspired by modern art, the experimental art that seeks new shapes and forms transgressing the limitations set by convention'. It became the dominant line of the 1960s. Interestingly, it

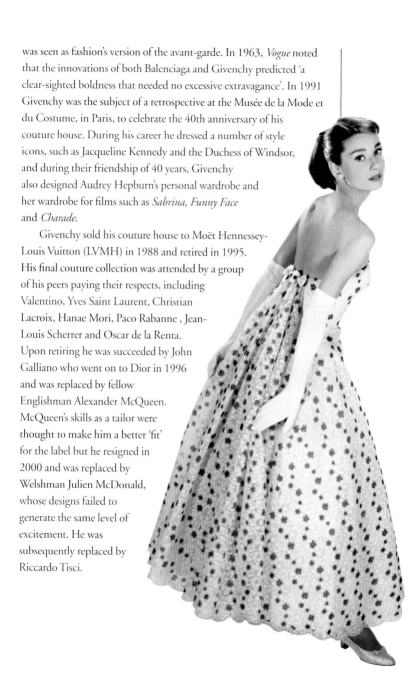

was seen as fashion's version of the avant-garde. In 1963, *Vogue* noted that the innovations of both Balenciaga and Givenchy predicted 'a clear-sighted boldness that needed no excessive extravagance'. In 1991 Givenchy was the subject of a retrospective at the Musée de la Mode et du Costume, in Paris, to celebrate the 40th anniversary of his couture house. During his career he dressed a number of style icons, such as Jacqueline Kennedy and the Duchess of Windsor, and during their friendship of 40 years, Givenchy also designed Audrey Hepburn's personal wardrobe and her wardrobe for films such as *Sabrina*, *Funny Face* and *Charade*.

Givenchy sold his couture house to Moët Hennessey-Louis Vuitton (LVMH) in 1988 and retired in 1995. His final couture collection was attended by a group of his peers paying their respects, including Valentino, Yves Saint Laurent, Christian Lacroix, Hanae Mori, Paco Rabanne , Jean-Louis Scherrer and Oscar de la Renta. Upon retiring he was succeeded by John Galliano who went on to Dior in 1996 and was replaced by fellow Englishman Alexander McQueen. McQueen's skills as a tailor were thought to make him a better 'fit' for the label but he resigned in 2000 and was replaced by Welshman Julien McDonald, whose designs failed to generate the same level of excitement. He was subsequently replaced by Riccardo Tisci.

Valentino

Dubbed the 'the sheikh of chic' by John Fairchild, editor of _Women's Wear Daily_ magazine, Valentino achieved an enduring nostalgic appeal with clothes that immortalised classic beauty; they spoke of wealth, glamour, refinement and elegance. His genius lay in the ease of the design, the stylistic fluidity and his perfect sense of proportion.

Born 1932, Voghers, Italy
Importance Infused fashion with classic beauty

Valentino opened his couture house in Rome in 1960, and became internationally renowned in the early 1970s. He acquired a very loyal clientele of glamorous, wealthy, European and American women who, in later years, were dubbed by _Women's Wear Daily_ as 'Val's Gals'. They included Jacqueline Onassis, baroness Marie Hélène de Rothschild, Madame Claude Pompidou, Pat Buckley, Nancy Kissinger, Grace Kelly, Elizabeth Taylor, Gina Lolobrigida, Marie Agnelli and Marissa Berenson. Valentino launched his ready-to-wear collection in Paris, 1969.

Immortalising Italian glamour, Valentino led the archetypal 'dolce vita'– as did his clients – and epitomised the 'high life' with a studio and flagship store overlooking the Spanish Steps in Rome. In 1968, he created his 'white' summer collection, which caused an instant sensation. Valentino admitted that he always loved white and he coupled his garments with embroidered white stockings that looked like lace. From this point on, white became a running theme in his collections. It was at this time

'I am not trendy. Trendy is for extremely young people…What I try to do is…glamorous, sexy, extremely feminine – but not clothes that only last for a short, short season.'

that his career grew strongest and his fashions went global. It was also when he attracted the attention of one of his most influential clients, Jackie Kennedy Onassis. When she chose to wear his white suit with embroidered 'Vs' on the bodice and matching shoes, the concept of the 'house logo' emerged.

Valentino admired the look of impeccably dressed, beautiful women who were feminine and confident in themselves. His work was never influenced by other designers and his clients overwhelmingly describe the continuity of beauty in his work. His clothes are known for their attention to meticulous detail, including scalloped and cut-out hems, fur, lace and velvet trim, extravagant linings, raglan sleeves, ruffles, pattern and texture mixtures. His materials were always of the very highest quality and he often combined a number of disparate materials in the one outfit, such as lace with tweed.

His evening wear paid particular attention to surface decoration, often combining light, transparent fabrics with sections of beading or shimmering textiles. Over his career, Valentino became best known for 'Valentino red', his signature colour, which he used to best advantage in his extravagant evening gowns.

In 2000, Valentino was awarded a Lifetime Achievement Award at the American Fashion Awards, a country in which he had a great following. After 40 years in the business, Valentino commented that he had been very fortunate and that he 'wouldn't change anything' in his career. He retired in 2007 and was replaced by Alessandra Facchinetti.

Yves Saint Laurent

Yves Saint Laurent's work was dominted by 'change': fashion journalists loved to cover his collection showings as they knew that they would see novelty with each one. The diversity of theme seen in his designs was inspired by art, his travels, cultural events, theatre, popular culture and films. Significantly, he sensed that the women's trouser suit, for both daytime and evening wear, would become a major fashion statement for decades.

Born 1936, Oran, Algeria
Importance Introduced the trouser suit –'le smoking' – to the women's wardrobe
Died 2008, Paris, France

Yves Saint Laurent worked as Christian Dior's assistant for three years, during which time 50 out of 80 garments produced in a collection were his. In 1962, he opened his own couture house. His first independent collections were a break away from traditional haute couture and, in retrospect, were quite revolutionary. Like Elsa Schiaparelli, he challenged the seriousness of high fashion and referred to his collections as 'fun clothes'. His ranges mimicked the beatnik look of the 1950s with turtlenecked sweaters and black leather jackets, as seen in his 'Beat' collection (1960), gaiety and lavishness in the 'Gypsy Look', and the popular television show based on the tales of Robin Hood. His travels took him around the world and his 'African' collection (1967) displayed rows of beads revealing the flesh below.

Yves Saint Laurent was one of the first haute couture designers to openly acknowledge his interest in popular culture. He announced that his greatest influence came from the fashion in 'the street'. His combination of couture and street style led him to design, among other things, his hippie protest clothing complete with headband and fringe. His love of theatrical costuming, such as that seen in the ballet production of *Scheherazade* inspired his use of bold, exotic colours and rich brocades.

Paintings by Pablo Picasso and Henri Matisse held in his own private collection, and postmodern art movements like pop and op, motivated his 'Mondrian' dress of 1965, at a time when retrospective exhibitions were being held around the globe, and his friendship with Andy Warhol led to his 'Pop Art Look' of 1966.

Yves Saint Laurent acknowledged that he drew inspiration from Chanel with his garments maintaining simplicity of line and form. He had an innate ability to accessorise every garment perfectly to create a totally coordinated look. Like Chanel, he appropriated men's clothing to be worn by women, thereby attempting to break down out-moded views about gender. His most characteristic look (which became the look of the 1970s) was the midi trench coat worn over trousers. His outstanding legacy also includes his tuxedo suits for women called 'Le Smoking' (1966 to 1982). After 40 years in the business, Yves Saint Laurent retired in 2002. His parting words were: 'I feel immense sadness. We are putting an end to a 40-year-old love story.'

'If I had to choose one design among all I have created, it would be 'Le Smoking'. Every year since 1966, it has been part of my collection. In a sense it is the Yves Saint Laurent trademark.'

Christian Lacroix

Best known for his witty, daring and extraordinarily luxurious fabrics, Christian Lacroix's clothes were a riotous mix of colour, print and texture. He brought new life to couture during the 1980s, a decade epitomised by its decadence, musing that he 'was dressing a new generation of young beautiful women who want luxurious but witty clothes'.

Born 1951, Arles, France
Importance Introduced bouffant or 'pouf' cocktail dresses that became a 1980s party staple

Lacroix is described as a fashion historian, costumier and designer. His designs were deeply influenced by his home of Arles, primitive and naive painting, gypsies, bullfighting and folk costumes of the region. He also drew reference liberally from fashion history. Initially designing for Jean Patou for five years, he opened his own couture and ready-to-wear house in 1987, which was the first couture house to open in Paris since 1962.

Described in *Rolling Stone* magazine as 'the gimme decade', the 1980s were a period of gross materialism. Lacroix's work was a reflection of popular culture, combining embroidery, patchwork, fur, lace and prints in the one outfit to create a fashion 'pastiche'. His use of startling colours and extraordinary accessories became a fine way of advertising one's wealth and status in society, which had become excessively consumer-oriented by this time.

Bursting onto the scene in 1986 with his famous bouffant or 'pouf' cocktail dresses, Lacroix was awarded the *Dé d'Or* or the Golden Thimble, a prize awarded by the international press for the best couture collection of the year. His bubble skirts were quickly copied, both by other designers and the high street, and became a staple of the late 1980s society party scene. All of Lacroix's clothes were cut very precisely and outfits often included corsets, drapes, frills, ruffles, jewels and numerous other forms of decoration. Many of the fabrics in the couture line were one-off creations by crafts people and textile artists. As a darling of the fashion media, John Fairchild at *Women's Wear Daily* named Lacroix as one of the top six designers in 1989 and 'the' designer of 'over-the-top' design for the decade.

'I love to mix everything up for the sake of mixing…for me fashion is expressing your own deep individuality; that is why I have always done noticeable things.'

Lacroix has been compared to Karl Lagerfeld – both men were design geniuses, ambitious and witty – yet their designs were completely different. His first collection was seen as the most innovative statement since Christian Dior and Yves Saint Laurent. However, by the early 1990s, the lavishness of the previous decade, embodied in Lacroix's collections, could not be sustained and haute couture sales slumped.

Jean-Paul Gaultier

A world-renowned fashion designer, Jean-Paul Gaultier challenged orthodox notions of what constitutes femininity and sexual desire in fashion. He was greatly influenced by the street culture of London in the 1980s, and in punk in particular, and brought elements of this influence onto the catwalk.

Born 1952, Val-de-Marne, France
Importance Blurred the lines between gender, race and sexuality

Gaultier did not receive any formal training as a designer but sent his drawings to Pierre Cardin who hired him as an assistant in 1970. He presented his own collection in 1976 and, from 1981 on, was known as the 'enfant terrible' of French fashion. His collections drew upon street styles and popular culture and, as a result, developed a wide appeal, as he successfully brought high fashion to the masses. Gaultier designed the wardrobe for many motion pictures including Luc Besson's *The Fifth Element*, Pedro Almodovar's *Kika*, Peter Greenaway's *The Cook, the Thief, his Wife and her Lover* and Jean-Pierre Jeunet's *The City of Lost Children*.

As the themes of his collection showings were constantly changing boundaries of gender, race and sexuality, they were provocative and contained elements of political shock. He used undergarments to manipulate the shape of the body and to suggest eroticism. He experimented with the idea that clothing could be a form of body armour and could create new silhouettes. His most publicised work was the corset with the cone-shaped bra that he designed for Madonna for her *Blond Ambition* tour in 1990, as well as the wardrobe he designed for her *Confessions* tour in 2006.

'It's always the badly dressed people who are the most interesting.'

Gaultier shocked the fashion world with his use of skirts for men, especially kilts, in an attempt to question gender stereotyping. He consistently presented cross-dressing in his menswear collections. He offered an alternative view of male sexuality as his models strutted the stage with feather boas, corsets, bejewelled bodices, skintight trousers and furs. He was celebrated for his designs in New York's Metropolitan Museum of Art exhibition entitled 'Bravehearts – Men in skirts'. His use of unconventional models on the catwalk, either older men, full-figured women or pierced and heavily tattooed individuals, reinforced his reputation for social deviance and defiance.

Gaultier presents haute couture collections as well as prêt-à-porter collections each season and has joined Hermès to design their newly relaunched clothing line. He is also well-known for his extensive perfume range and, in 2005, his Gaultier[2] (pronounced Gaultier to the power of two) was advertised as a unisex 'fragrance for humanity', catering to both sexes.

Haute Couture

Giorgio Armani

When Giorgio Armani appeared on the cover of *Time* magazine on 5 April 1982, he was the first fashion designer to do so since Christian Dior, back in 1957. A huge influence on most contemporary menswear designers, Armani revolutionised corporate dress for both men and women during in the second half of the twentieth century.

Born 1934, Piacenza, Italy
Importance Revolutionised corporate dress for men and women

Questioning the function of men's clothing in the contemporary world when he launched his first menswear line in 1974, Armani developed a new style based on an understated casual lifestyle. He deconstructed, re-cut, reshaped and re-proportioned the male suit using softer, more languid fabrics, eliminating any superfluous details. His men's suits have become the ultimate symbol of sensuality coupled with confidence, rather than power.

When he launched his womenswear line in 1975, Armani anticipated the second wave of the women's liberation movement, which culminated in the 1980s. He designed a masculinised, look for women, creating daytime clothes that were renowned for their cut, simplicity and use of luxurious fabrics. He combined masculine cutting techniques with languid, soft, feminine fabrics, and invented the new 'power suit' for women. He changed the shape of the armhole, simplified the finishing details and used fabrics made up of seven or

'I design for real people. I think of our customers all the time. There is no virtue whatsoever in creating clothing or accessories that are not practical.'

eight different coloured threads in the weave, to create a soft, muted colour that was hard to define.

Dubbed 'Mr Hollywood', Armani created the androgynous look for women when Diane Keaton wore his clothes in the film, *Annie Hall* (1977). He reinvented the idea of celebrity dressing and achieved worldwide fame by dressing Richard Gere in the 1980 film *American Gigolo*. The list of Hollywood stars that currently wear Armani almost exclusively include Tom Cruise, George Clooney, Martin Scorsese, Jodie Foster and Cate Blanchett, among others. Armani's evening wear for women is known for its exquisite beading, diaphanous materials and pattern layering, underlining his reputation for style, sophistication and glamour.

Like Pierre Cardin, Armani was a pioneer in the launch of cheaper diffusion lines – 'Mani' and *Le Collezione* (1979), *Emporio Armani* (1981), 'Armani Jeans' (1981) and 'A/X Armani Express' (1991). He expanded his business empire in 2000 with the launch of 'Armani Casa Homewares', a cosmetics line and a new haute couture range called *Armani Prive* (2005), which predominantly consisted of red carpet evening wear. The Guggenheim Museum in New York launched a retrospective exhibition of Armani's work in October 2000, which travelled the world.

Haute Couture

STREET STYLE

'Street style' is one of the very few trends that are resistant to the stereotype of globalised fashion. The term refers to fashion that has been influenced by young people who are drawn to new fads and alternative lifestyles. It is a style of dressing that is generated from the ground upwards, rather than the top down. In the 1960s, Yves Saint Laurent was one of the first designers to claim that he was directly inspired by what was being worn by the younger generation on the streets of London.

Since the 1920s, when high fashion began its long process of 'democratisation' through mass production and the rise of ready-to-wear, there have been many significant factors that have contributed to the advent of street style. Among these are a number of factors that haute couture designers introduced themselves, and which contributed to a decline in elitist notions of what constituted 'good taste'. For example, Coco Chanel introduced jersey for daytime womenswear, yet previously it was considered suitable only for men's underwear, while Elsa Schiaparelli used common images such as animals, circus acrobats and coffee beans as buttons in her haute couture clothing.

Fashion as a form of protest emerged in the 1950s, greatly influenced by the Hollywood film industry. Movies, starring James Dean and Marlon Brando, immortalised the cult of the tough, anti-heroes who wore blue jeans and black leather jackets covered in studs. Popular culture was reinforced in the 1960s when 'everyday' images had an effect on art and fashion. The art of the supermarket, comic strip, billboards and television infiltrated the arena of 'highbrow' culture. Clothing became a symbol of protest. Groups within society, extracting themselves from the mainstream and dressing accordingly, were referred to as 'subcultures'. The hippie movement, reinforced by the Woodstock 'love-in', illustrated that Indian headbands and beads, personalised jeans worn with cheesecloth tops, or long peasant-like dresses and sandals, signalled a rejection of social values. It was a form of self-expression, and the clothing became symbolic.

By the late 1970s, a shift towards a more aggressive form of street style appeared in London with the emergence of 'punk'. It culminated in the 1980s and 1990s, expressing hostility to political and social institutions through body piercings, tattoes and multicoloured hair or shaved heads. And it was this form of visual protest that became adopted by high fashion and the middle-class bourgeousie for over two decades.

In more recent times, street style refers to the trends that have been expressed by youth in Japan, specifically in the Harajuku section of Tokyo. In the 1990s, Japanese youth adopted a type of dress-up style, infusing multiple looks and styles to create a unique form of dress, which made reference to a variety of themes including Gothic Lolita, the witch-look, the cowgirl look, and the cute look (Kawaii). It is a combination of street culture and individualistic creativity, free from the limitations of conformity, with an emphasis on self-expression through individual styling, combining plaids, T-shirts, ripped clothing and studded accessories. It is a form of 'style surfing'. For some, identity is something that can be changed as often as you change what you are wearing. Harajuku street style is promoted in Japanese and international publications such as *Kera, Tune, Gothic & Lolita Bible* and *Fruits*, and it has inspired many prominent designers and fashion ideals.

Emilio Pucci

More of a fabric designer than a clothing designer, Emilio Pucci is one of the great Italian contributors to the success of Italian post-war design. Renowned for his fine silk clothes, he found inspiration for his colourful signature prints and scarves in the flags that he saw as a child in Siena. Synonymous with the Mediterranean lifestyle, his colours and prints were based on shades of fuchsia, turquoise, ultramarine, sea-green and lemon-yellow. He is credited with the invention of 'Capri' pants.

Born 1914, Florence, Italy
Importance Raised status of post-war Italian design with colourful silk prints
Died 1992, Florence, Italy

The first Pucci shop was established in Capri in 1949 and, during the 1950s and 1960s, the name became recognised among the international jet set as a purveyor of fine silk clothes in signature patterns and colours. Like Gucci, Pucci's simple clothing pieces best highlighted the fabric and pattern – usually bold prints in swirling abstract patterns and acidic colours. His clothing design centred on sports and resort wear, including elegant tapered trouser suits, shirts, and bias cut, v-neck, silk-jersey shift dresses.

Pucci's first foray into fashion was as early as 1947, when he designed skiwear using stretch fabric. His work was published the following winter in a special feature in *Harper's Bazaar*. The sleekness of the fabric caused a great stir and, consequently, Pucci designed a stretch swimwear line (1949). Numerous offers from American manufacturers followed, but he instead set up an haute couture boutique in the fashionable resort of Canzone del Mare on the island of Capri, and a second boutique in Rome. He expanded his range to include brightly coloured, bold-patterned silk scarves, stretch blouses and wrinkle-free, printed-silk dresses. By the mid 1950s, he had gained international recognition.

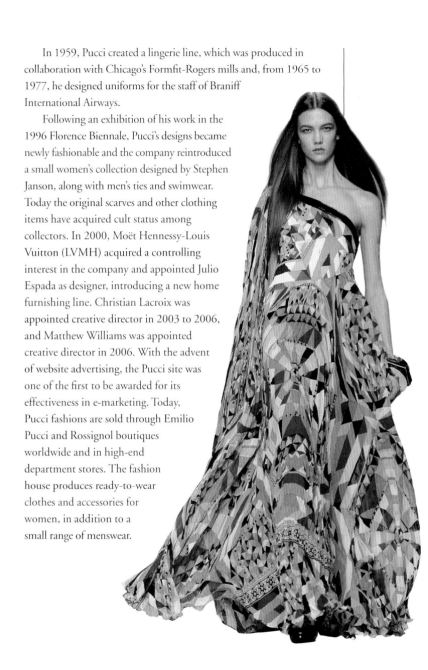

In 1959, Pucci created a lingerie line, which was produced in collaboration with Chicago's Formfit-Rogers mills and, from 1965 to 1977, he designed uniforms for the staff of Braniff International Airways.

Following an exhibition of his work in the 1996 Florence Biennale, Pucci's designs became newly fashionable and the company reintroduced a small women's collection designed by Stephen Janson, along with men's ties and swimwear. Today the original scarves and other clothing items have acquired cult status among collectors. In 2000, Moët Hennessy-Louis Vuitton (LVMH) acquired a controlling interest in the company and appointed Julio Espada as designer, introducing a new home furnishing line. Christian Lacroix was appointed creative director in 2003 to 2006, and Matthew Williams was appointed creative director in 2006. With the advent of website advertising, the Pucci site was one of the first to be awarded for its effectiveness in e-marketing. Today, Pucci fashions are sold through Emilio Pucci and Rossignol boutiques worldwide and in high-end department stores. The fashion house produces ready-to-wear clothes and accessories for women, in addition to a small range of menswear.

Mary Quant

Mary Quant responded to the youth culture of London's Carnaby Street during the 'Swinging Sixties', recognising its need for bright, bouncy, playful clothing. Like Chanel, she designed garments of simple shape and construction that were comfortable to wear. She also placed emphasis on the 'total look' which, for Quant, meant considering underwear, cosmetics, shoes, bags and jewellery to match.

Born 1934, Kent, England
Importance Exploited the youth revolution of the 1960s

Quant designed for the young, producing 'off-the-peg' clothes that parodied childlike garments such as short pinafores, tunics, pleated skirts with braces, knickerbockers, playsuits and crazy coloured tights. She combined bright, outrageous colours in zany patterns and introduced flannel as an evening material. She turned fashion upside-down, combining checked fabrics with polka dots, using satins for short sets, and creating fun handbags with shoulder straps and decorated with large daisies. Nothing was sacred in fashion terms – the 'baby-boomers' were prepared to break all the rules.

While Quant had no formal training in dressmaking or couture, she was a designer who trained at art school and was not afraid to defy mainstream ideas. She established Chelsea's first fashion boutique, 'Bazaar', in 1955, which catered for the new buying power of the young, and capitalised on fast-fad turnover. Quant changed her styling every six weeks – a stark contrast to the existing policy of showing couture collections twice yearly. It signalled the significant shift from couture design to ready-to-wear in this post-war period.

In 1964, Quant introduced history's shortest skirt – the 'Mini' – made from easy-care synthetic fabrics that were suitable for an active life. Her marketing was aimed at the working girl, who was prepared to spend her budget on the 'latest look' every payday. As an astute business entrepreneur, Quant produced designs for Butterick Patterns in 1964 to enable her styling to reach a larger market – the home sewers. With the new technological sewing machines available in the 1960s, increased numbers of women were returning to home sewing, as the simplicity of flat pattern pieces (no gathers or pleats) made garment-making a simple, straightforward alternative. Quant also produced a cosmetic line that complemented the colours she chose for her clothes. Glossy eye shadows, cheek blushers and lipsticks were made in purple-reds, tangerine-pinks and mauve-blue colours.

Quant was concerned with all aspects of design, manufacture and distribution as well as the promotion of her products. While she initially made her own clothing for the boutique, she turned quickly to mass-production methods, which were the basis of the ready-to-wear industry. Instead of presenting deadly serious and subdued fashion shows, she had her models hop, skip and jump down the catwalks or photographed in 'tourist locations' around London. This not only promoted her label but promoted Britain as well. In her new approach to fashion retailing, Quant became a major contributor to this shift. She was awarded an OBE in 1966 for her contribution to the British fashion industry.

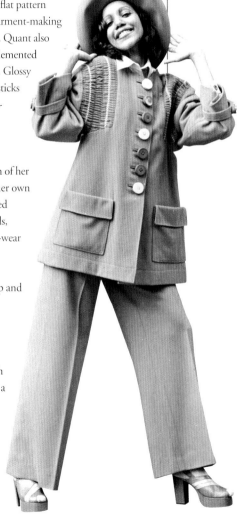

André Courrèges

André Courrèges studied civil engineering before entering the fashion world and shaped his garments into stylised, futuristic, architectural forms. Producing highly sophisticated work, based on exquisite cutting and structural techniques, his designs were devoid of any superfluous embellishment, and it was this absolute, streamlined simplicity that became his signature style.

Born 1923, Pau, France
Importance Brought an architectural structure to dress

Courrèges' 'ultramodern' salon and his innovative fashion parades reinforced the cutting-edge, space-age nature of his collections. His parades became a type of performance where theatre, music and fashion mixed. His interiors were all white, stark and minimalist and his models walked in a robot-like movement wearing helmets not unlike those worn by astronauts. It was a time when new interactive theatrical practice was being introduced in many avant-garde productions. In terms of marketing, the performance became as important as the clothes themselves.

The A-line dress, first introduced by Christian Dior, became the main shape of the 1960s. Courrèges gave his garments this triangular flare and used mainly white and pastel colours in his range, developing a universally recognised styling through cut, fabric, colour and detail. Jacqueline Kennedy immortalised the Courrèges look in the 1960s, wearing his above-the-knee, triangular-shaped pastel coats with matching pillbox hats and flat-heeled shoes. He held his first collection showing in 1961 and his dream was to bring his designs within easy reach of modern young women, not exclusively rich couturier clients. Courrèges preferred gaberdine as a fabric, as it held its sculptural shape and its surface enhanced the channel stitching that became his trademark. This stitching was used both as a functional and aesthetic technique, as it provided a means of creating abstract patterns on the surface of the cloth. Furthermore, the welted seams highlighted the simplicity of the construction of the clothing. Many of his garments were banded at the hem with a strip of white fabric which further defined the silhouette. Courrèges' colours were called spinach-green, caramel and tomato. White mid-calf 'Copy' boots, which were flat heeled to make the wearer feel youthful, were the main accessory.

Andre Courrèges had worked as an apprentice to Cristóbal Balenciaga, the master tailor, for 11 years. While Balenciaga's influence was a major contributor to his work, Courrèges' 1964 collection was his fashion turning point. He introduced short mini-length skirts (the same year as Mary Quant) and showed the barest backs in Paris. He began to design women's trousers for all occasions, including gala evening functions. Legendary was an evening trouser suit made of white lace, which covered the front of the body but was only secured at the nape of the neck. Courrèges often designed clothes for wear without bras, as the curve of the breast was accentuated by the cut of the bodice. He cut waists low, baring midriffs, in what was considered an anti-feminine trend at the time.

In his attempt to cater for the modern young woman, Courrèges brought out a large ready-to-wear collection that was widely exported. In 1965, he held his first haute couture show and, in the same year, began establishing workshops to create clothes at 'boutique prices' for direct marketing. Over the years, his style changed little, but his work, catered to the 'youth quake' that dominated the decade.

Paco Rabanne

Preferring 'engineer' to 'designer', Paco Rabanne was fascinated with the new products and materials that emerged as a result of war technologies. Breaking away from traditional couture, he invented a new approach to garment fabrication. He experimented with such unconventional materials as metal, paper and plastic and combined knits, leather and fur together. Instead of using fabrics, he used geometric plastic and metal pieces to make garments that were linked together.

Born 1934, San Sebastian, Spain
Importance Introduced radical materials to fashion design

The son of one of Cristóbal Balenciaga's seamstresses, Rabanne studied architecture before starting a fashion career designing jewellery for Givenchy, Christian Dior and Balenciaga. He opened his couturier salon in 1966; a time when popular culture greatly impacted society and change was the order of the day. His first couturier collection was entitled 'Twelve Unwearable Dresses' and featured garments made from phosphorescent plastic discs strung on metal wire; they became the most influential dresses of the 1960s. It was estimated that, by 1966, Rabanne was using 30,000 metres (32,500 yards) of rhodoid plastic per month for his garments and jewellery.

When Rabanne exhausted the possibilities of plastic, he created another version of chain mail, where tiny triangles of aluminium and leather were held together using flexible wire rings. From this, he constructed a series of minidresses. The garments resembled sculpture or pieces of body jewellery and inadvertently strengthened the link between art and fashion.

While Rabanne's garments gave the appearance of being heavy, in reality, they were very light and this visual paradox became a major characteristic of postmodern design in the 1960s. One outfit was made in three parts – the hood and shoulder cowl, the bodice and the trousers – yet, in its entirety, it looked exactly like a seamless medieval suit of armour. As the 'see-through' look was a major feature of the 1960s, body stockings were worn underneath these garments for modesty's sake.

Rabanne's revolutionary methods inspired both his contemporaries and followers for decades. In particular, fellow designer, Emanuel Ungaro, used atypical materials to make body coverings that doubled as clothing. He used a range of materials from paper to platinum. This use of non-traditional materials was significant, as it not only represented a break with traditional couture, but also indicated that boundaries between different media genres were breaking down in fashion as they were in art.

Fads in fashion were short-lived in the 1960s as permanence and durability were no longer of any concern. Scott Paper commissioned Rabanne to make paper dresses to complement his plastic and metal creations, and they were paraded on the catwalks of Paris. While this was seen mainly as a 'fun' activity – another feature of postmodern design – it is still surprising to appreciate fully the impact that paper clothing had on society. The Beatles wore neon-orange paper jackets on a tour to Los Angeles, Air India's hostesses wore paper saris and the rich and famous wore paper outfits to numerous 'paper' balls and dinners that were held during this decade.

Pierre Cardin

Despite his disastrous sense of timing, Pierre Cardin became a very successful designer and a major name in fashion in the 1960s. Fascinated with technology, and using materials such as vinyl, studs and giant zips, his clothing epitomised the look of this techno-inspired decade. He had a passion for architectural shapes including the diamond, circle and rectangle, and much of his work reflected the classical simplicity of formalism, reminiscent of the 1920s Bauhaus era.

Born 1922, San Biagio di Callalta, Italy
Importance A master of pleating and a great business entrepreneur

A number of Cardin's major innovations, such as his 'Maxi' coat and his 1966 tweed pinafores with polo-necked sweaters were not adopted until the 1970s, and had a very short lifespan. Nevertheless, he enjoyed tremendous success. He created extraordinary collars, which were often large, double-layered and with pronounced seaming that created the surface pattern. Geometric detail was another of his trademarks and his sleek and simple designs were reminiscent of the bold, graphic art movements of the day.

Cardin was an expert with materials. Like Madeleine Vionnet, he became fascinated with pleating, cowl drapery and using fabric cut on the bias, experimenting extensively with various technical possibilities. He preferred to use wool crêpe or wool jersey to create a soft, supple and nonchalant look. Some of his most beautiful bias garments became known as 'spiralling' dresses, which used finely pleated fabric, either with scalloped or appliquéd edging. He became a perfectionist, showing great mastery with pleats – especially sunray, pencil and cartridge pleats – which he used in collars, sleeves and godets (fabric panels).

In 1961, he opened his first men's boutique and soon became a world leader in menswear. He designed the popular high-buttoned and collarless 'Nehru' jacket for casual wear and double-breasted shirts for evening wear. He specialised in trouser suits, which were often accompanied with matching hoods. He became well-known for his futuristic styling. His 'Moon Range' of 1964 (years ahead of the moon landings) featured brief tabards worn over catsuits, along with high leather boots and space helmets. In 1966, his sculptural, moulded dresses, worn with coloured stockings to match, were very successful lines and became the look of the decade. Both André Courrèges and Cardin used austere, minimalist styling to capitalise on the space-age theme and to reflect the ultra-modern lifestyle that emerged at this time.

Cardin was the first of the postwar designers to sign licensing contracts in which other manufacturers produced the clothes and used his label. As the licensing contracts expanded, his name became synonymous with a range of products including belts, ties, shoes, hats, towels, bed sheets and other household goods.

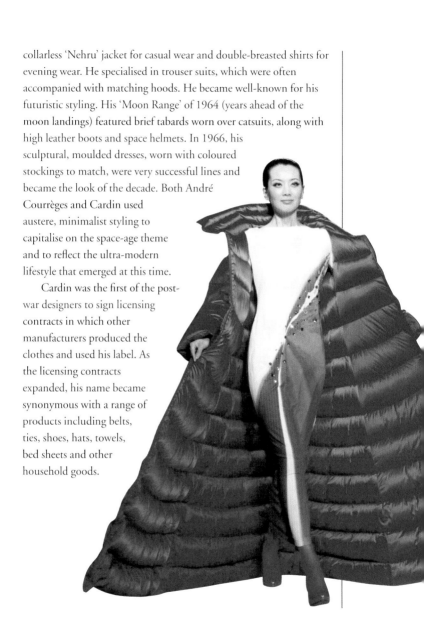

Zandra Rhodes

Zandra Rhodes' controversial 'Conceptual Chic' collection of 1977 capitalised on a growing fascination with punk fashion, an emerging street-style trend. This appropriation of punk culture was adopted by numerous other designers of the day, including Vivienne Westwood. In social terms, it further underlined the changes in attitude towards elitist practices in society and in fashion, in particular.

Born 1940, Kent, England
Importance Among the first designers to capitalise on punk

Rhodes' mother was a fitter in a Paris fashion house and this gave Zandra her interest in designing clothes. She studied textile design at Medway College of Art and the Royal College of Art in London. Like Mary Quant, she established a small boutique called the Fulham Road Clothes Shop where she made up her own garments. A perfectionist, she thoroughly researched every aspect of the particular theme that she was inspired by, whether it was for her Zebra collection, 'North American Indian' collection or 'Ayers Rock' collection.

She made detailed drawings and colour studies before starting to design specific textiles for each range. Like Yves Saint Laurent, her diversity of influences, came from history, nature, her travels, street styles and from other designers. Her beautiful textile designs were labour-intensive, with fabrics being hand-dyed, beaded and embroidered. This emphasis on individuality and uniqueness in design was indicative of 1960s artistic trends.

Rhodes became well-known for her hand-painted chiffon ethnic dresses and her 'Chinese', 'Shell' and 'Butterfly' collections. Her work appealed to 'alternative thinkers' of every age group and, like Elsa Schiaparelli, she consolidated the link between fashion and art. In 1973, Cecil Beaton chose fashion photographs of her clothes for inclusion in his retrospective fashion photography exhibition held at the Victoria and Albert Museum, London.

With the arrival of punk, Rhodes brought out her own version of glamorous ripped and torn garments, carefully hand-edged and pinned together with 18-carat-gold safety pins purchased from Cartier Jewellers. Ironically, this anti-establishment youth revolution that emerged from the back streets was not only embraced by British high fashion, but was adopted globally by the fashion industry. In social terms, this highlighted the increasing changes in attitude towards elitist practices, particularly in fashion.

Zandra Rhodes has designed striking costumes for the British rock group Queen; a beautiful pink and white chiffon, handkerchief-hemmed dress weighted down with glass and pearls for Diana, Princess of Wales (worn to Japan on a state visit); a crinoline dress for Princess Anne's official engagement photograph; and an Elizabethan-inspired gown, which she herself wore to a party at Buckingham Palace (held by the Queen and Prince Philip to honour the achievements of British creative icons).

In 2003, Rhodes opened a Fashion and Textile Museum in what had been an old warehouse in East London. The first exhibition was entitled 'My Favourite Dress', and showed dresses from 70 designers including Galliano, McQueen, Lacroix, Missoni and Ungaro. In 2005, the first retrospective show of her own work was mounted.

FASHION MAGAZINES

Traditionally, changes in fashion were conveyed throughout Europe via engraved and coloured illustrations in periodicals, which, by the end of the eighteenth century, had become quite numerous. In fact, it seemed that changes in fashion became more rapid with the increased numbers of these publications, as they were lavishly illustrated and attracted much attention.

By the middle of the nineteenth century, fashion journals began to highlight the work of individual designers, such as the couturier Charles Frederick Worth, who were attempting to create an identifiable style that catered for a particular clientele. In England, *Queen's* began circulation in 1861, with *Harper's* (now *Harper's Bazaar*) following in 1867, both very influential publications. America's first fashion magazine, *Weldon's Ladies Journal*, published in 1875, and Australia's *The Home Journal* in 1920, included paper patterns in the price, which encouraged home dressmaking, particularly for women living in remote, rural areas.

In Paris, Lucien Vogel published a number of fashion journals including *Jardin des Modes, Les Feuillets d'Art, L'Illustration des Modes* but the most famous was *La Gazette du Bon Temps,* which was published from 1912 to 1925 (with a break of some years during the war) when it was purchased by *Vogue*. Vogel has been applauded for his taste and imagination in producing journals which were of a standard which has rarely been equalled. *La Gazette du Bon Temps* was a lavish publication printed on thick, handmade paper. Well-known writers were commissioned to add articles on fashion or on some event of the day (often about the Ballets Russes). The illustrations were very stylised and based on abstract forms with flat areas of colour that created idealised versions of the clothing featured. Leading illustrators of the day contributing to the magazine included Paul Iribe, Georges Lepape, Benito, Pierre Brissaud, André Edouard Marty and Raoul Dufy. There were rival publications competing with *La Gazette,* including *Femina, Le Journal des Dames* and *Modes et Manières d'Aujourdhui,* but during the First World War many were forced to close their doors due to a shortage of paper and manpower.

Vogue was founded by Arthur Baldwin Turnure in 1892, and purchased by Condé Nast in 1909. There are now 18 editions published world-wide not only featuring fashion but writings on art, culture, and ideas. When *Vogue* and *Harper's Bazaar* began publishing, it became their policy to continue using drawings on the front cover, with Lepape and Benito working for *Vogue* and Erté for *Harper's Bazaar*. During the latter part of the 1920s and 1930s, photographs by George Hoyningen-Huené, Horst P. Horst, Edward Steichen or Man Ray became more popular. There were a growing number of fashion journals published in the post-war years, and more sophisticated methods of communication and advertising emerged.

Owing to economic restraints following the war, elite journals like *Vogue* began to run special features on 'Dressing on a Low Budget' and 'How to Reconstruct your Clothes'. *Vogue* had an image as an exclusive magazine, but by the 1920s it was making a concerted effort to appeal to a broader audience by increasing its general appeal.

Fashion magazine editors have become powerful celebrities in their own right. They have been the arbiters of fashion directions and have been instrumental in determining the fate of many designers, photographers and illustrators during the course of the twentieth century. Names such as Edna Woolman Chase, Diana Vreeland and the present editor, Anna Wintour (American *Vogue*), Alex Brodovich and Liz Tiberis (*Harper's Bazaar*) and, of course, Condé Nast, have become immortalised.

Guccio Gucci

Guccio Gucci, while working in the kitchen of the Ritz Hotel in London, noticed that the wealthy patrons had their initials stamped into their luggage. As a stroke of genius, he decided to stamp the, now famous, Gucci initials onto his leather goods. Instantly a sign of status and quality, this Gucci labelling was possibly one of the first branding insignias that was used in fashion accessories.

Born 1881, Florence, Italy
Importance Introduced one of the first branding insignias used in fashion accessories
Died 1953, Florence, Italy

The House of Gucci was founded in Florence, Italy, in 1921. Emerging out of a saddlery business, started by Guccio Gucci in 1906, the firm initially retailed fashion accessories. Gucci opened his first store in Florence in 1921, selling equestrian-inspired leather accessories and luggage. The first signature bag, the 'Bamboo' bag, named because of its signature bamboo handles, was created in the 1940s and is still in production today. Owing to leather shortages after the Second World War, the iconic double G motif was introduced on canvas, and this was followed, in the 1950s, by the distinctive red and green banding stripe that Gucci placed on all suitcases, bags, satchels, wallets and purses – a trademark that became the most copied emblem in the world.

In this post-war period, the Gucci company grew to international proportions and expanded its range to include clothing, perfume and household goods as well as accessories. This proved to be a disadvantage in later years, as the company found it difficult to sustain legal costs incurred in trying to protect its copyright against a proliferation of imitations flooding the market. When Guccio Gucci died in 1953, his sons Aldo, Vasco, Ugo and Rodolpho took control.

By the 1960s, another iconic piece of merchandise, the Gucci loafer, with its signature gilt 'snaffle' trim, became a status symbol in its own right. Within a decade, Gucci became a household name

'Quality is remembered long after the price is forgotten.'

synonymous with the international jet set. While the reputation of the fashion house suffered in the 1980s, owing to excessive licensing and bitter family feuds, its trendy cachet was resurrected with the introduction of the Gucci 'clog' in the early 1990s, which became the bestselling item in the summer of 1993 and was the most copied shoe of the season. This re-established the Gucci name as a serious contender in the high-fashion stakes and fused its name, once again, among luxury products.

The transformation of the Gucci brand had started in 1989 with the appointment of an American, Dawn Mello, as executive vice president and creative director. She was followed in the mid-1990s by Domenico De Sole, who then became the CEO. Tom Ford was appointed head designer in 1994 and he resurrected the company's image and fortunes. By reinterpreting the company classics and infusing them with a sexy, 1970s glamour, Ford was able to capture the fashion zeitgeist.

In 1998 Prada acquired a portion of Gucci stocks, but Gucci consolidated its business position by forming a strategic partnership with the Pinault Printemps Redoute group. In 2002, Frida Giannini, previously a bag designer for Fendi, joined Gucci's accessory department, contributing bold reinventions of house signatures as part of Ford's team, before becoming Creative Director in 2005 following the success of her relaunch of the Flora print as a bag collection.

Karl Lagerfeld

A self-proclaimed fashion nymphomaniac, Karl Lagerfeld is a stylist of extraordinary talent, and the most prolific and high-profile designer working today. He has taken on the 'persona' of numerous other designer brands and created successful signature looks for all of them. He was also the first designer to set about rejuvenating iconic brands, such as Chanel, which he did to great acclaim.

Born 1938, Hamburg, Germany
Importance
Rejuvenated the House of Chanel to great acclaim

In 1954, aged just 16, Lagerfeld won top prize for a woman's coat design entered in the International Wool Secretariat (Yves Saint Laurent won the dress category). He started as a design assistant at Pierre Balmain (1955–1958) and became head designer at Jean Patou from 1958–1963. In the same year, he joined the newly formed ready-to-wear business of Chloé and put himself and the fashion house on the map, making it one of the hottest labels of the 1970s. For Chloé, his love of art-deco styling came to the fore in the cut and patterning of fabrics. Under his direction, the house became known for its light, layered, flowing, feminine clothes, often unlined and free of extraneous detail. The clothes were predominantly made from fabrics such as crêpe de Chine and chiffon. In 1975 Lagerfeld started designing for Fendi, in Rome, and continues to do so to this day.

It is however for Chanel, for whom he started designing in 1983, that he is best known today. At the time he was, perhaps, the world's most famous designer. He completely reinvented the image of the house, catering for a new, youthful market and, in the process, Chanel has become among the most innovative and recognised labels in the world. Lagerfeld has paid homage to endless variations on the signature Chanel look, by mixing in references from past collections and contemporary street style. He broadened shoulders, shortened hemlines and introduced new materials such as leather, denim, terry cloth and stretch fabrics. He exaggerated the size of the classic Chanel accessories, such as gold chains and pearls, and poked fun at her millinery by using images of armchairs and pastry tarts. While he has, at times, been accused of 'dumbing down' and 'vulgarising' the style of the house, under his direction it has become one of the most innovative, relevant and glamorous labels on the fashion scene today. For Lagerfeld, humour plays a vital part in the fashion process. His version of Chanel's little black dress was lavishly decorated with a wealth of *trompe l'oeil* jewellery embroidery. This was in response to Chanel's comment that 'to be elaborate is easy, to create the ultimate simplicity (the little black dress) is difficult'.

'Nothing should look serious…everything should have a light touch.'

Lagerfeld opened his own fashion business in 1984 and his own brands include the short-lived Lagerfeld Gallery and the current KL, both owned by the Tommy Hilfiger Company. As well as designing, Lagerfeld has hosted a number of fashion documentaries and indulges a passion for photography (often directing and photographing the advertising campaigns for the labels he designs). He has also established a small publishing company that specialises in photography, art and architecture. 'Lagerfeld Confidential', a documentary on the designer directed by Rudolphe Marconi, was released in 2006 and provides a unique and illuminating glimpse into his peripatetic life.Another documentary was also released in 2007, 'Un roi seul', directed by Thierry Demaiziere and Alban Teurlai.

Gianni Versace

One of the first fashion designers to embrace the concept of the supermodel, Oscar-winning Gianni Versace developed an aura of both opulence and decadence in his designs that appealed to the very wealthy (or those wanting to feel very wealthy). Today, the internationally-branded company, known for its label featuring a golden head of Medusa, is celebrated for its flamboyant, glitzy, hedonistic and overtly sexual clothing.

Born 1946, Calabria, Italy
Importance Champion of the supermodel
Died 1997, Miami, USA

Having founded his company in 1978, Gianni Versace became one of the biggest labels of the 1980s. Dubbed 'rock and roll chic', his clothing combined silks, fine chain mail and pliant metallic mesh, leather and denim and plenty of beading. His evening garments were synonymous with luxury and extravagance, despite the fact that his clothes were cut very simply, often on the bias, and always close to the body to both define and reveal. Elizabeth Hurley caused a sensation when she wore a black Versace evening dress to the 1994 premier of *Four Weddings and a Funeral*; almost completely sliced down the sides, the dress was joined with large safety pins.

Milan had been established as Italy's fashion capital by the mid 1970s, and Italian designers continued to be acknowledged for their specialist use of textiles. The patterns of Versace's textiles in particular are reminiscent of classical and Renaissance periods, Italian baroque and futurism. Not afraid to

'My inspiration is not scholarly, it is more instinctive. I always look ahead. The past is just an excuse for experiments. Classical means contemporary to me'

use bold colours or patterns, and with some textiles influenced by the 1960s op art period (a genre of visual art, especially painting, that makes use of optical illusions), his work appealed to a number of celebrity clients including Princess Diana, Bruce Springstein, Elton John, Sting, Prince, Eric Clapton and George Michael. He also designed costumes for the theatre and films.

When grunge became chic, with its shabby-looking clothes, Versace featured a version of psychedelic grunge in his Milan menswear show in spring 1993. An astute businessman, he launched breathtakingly sexy advertising campaigns with photographs taken by Richard Avedon and Bruce Weber. He was one of the first designers to truly embrace the idea of the supermodel, and his collections often featured Claudia Schiffer, Christy Turlington, Linda Evangelista, Cindy Crawford, Naomi Campbell, Carla Bruni and Helena Christiansen. When he was criticised for his ultra-sexy clothing, he turned his collection around and replied that he 'dressed Claudia Schiffer and Madonna like my mother used to dress'. After his untimely death, his sister Donatella took over as head designer and his brother Santo controlled the company's financial affairs.

SUPERMODELS

The supermodel era of the 1980s and early 1990s was a golden age for the fashion industry. This period produced a wave of supermodels, the most famous being Linda Evangelista, Naomi Campbell, Cindy Crawford, Christie Turlington and Tatjana Patitz, whose faces appeared together on the cover of *Vogue* in 1990. They were treated like celebrities, and became more famous than the designers whose clothes they wore. They were perceived as the new goddesses of glamour and they contributed to making the couture houses even more famous.

The rise of the fashion model to the status of the 'supermodel' has a long history, with Paul Poiret being the first couturier to take his five models on a fashion parade tour of America in 1913 (although they were not allowed to speak to the press or potential buyers under any circumstance). Before this, at the turn of the twentieth century, early haute couture designers used their wives as their models, or employed women to work in-house, showing their collections to select clients.

When the international haute couture and prêt-à-porter collections were paraded on a much wider scale, in collective venues organised by the Chambre Syndicale, a much larger contingency of models was required. It was at this point that models began wearing clothes for a number of different fashion houses and, subsequently, gained popularity as individual models. Those in the highest demand were also the highest paid and they rapidly gained a reputation as superstars of the catwalk.

Gianni Versace is one of the designers widely credited for creating the supermodel phenomenon of the 1990s. Subsequently, Grace Jones was a favoured model for Azzedine Alaia when he won two fashion Oscars in 1985; Inès de la Fressange was the official model for Chanel in the 1980s; in the 1990s it was Claudia Schiffer and, reportedly, she received the highest pay for modelling in 2002; Kate Moss became the face of the 1990s, her childlike innocence attracting designers such as John Galliano, who offered her the first catwalk appearance in 1989, and Calvin Klein, who used her to promote his perfume range in the early 1990s.

Linda Evangelista, who first appeared in French *Vogue* in 1987, is still one of the most sought-after models by fashion designers. Having retired for three years between 1998 and 2001, Evangelista re-emerged into the modelling world, and was featured in 28 pages of American *Vogue* in their September issue. Like a chameleon, she altered her appearance every few months by changing the colour of her hair. The famous fashion photographer, Peter Lindbergh, persuaded her to cut her long hair short in 1988 and in the following six months she appeared on the covers of every international edition of *Vogue*.

The average career of a model ranged from ten years in the 1950s and 1960s, to five years in the 1970s and 1980s. In the 1990s and early twenty-first century, high-profile careers can sometimes last just a few years. Top designers are now also using actresses to promote their products, as they are seen more frequently by the public in movies and on the front covers of magazines. Nicole Kidman, for example, has become the face of Chanel for the perfume Chanel No. 5 as she epitomises the image of class and propriety that the parfumerie wants to project, while Keira Knightley is the face of Chanel for the perfume Coco Mademoiselle.

Ralph Lauren

With an innate ability to respond to American conservatism, Ralph Lauren has perfected the landed-gentry image of quality, tradition and prestige, producing fashion that exudes simplicity, versatility and comfort in clothing. His work promotes nostalgia and he transmits this image in the homey wood-panelled low-light interiors of his shops. His goods sell at prices that upper middle class Americans can afford. This winning formula, coupled with his all-American good looks, has made him one of the leading ready-to-wear designers in the world.

Born 1939, New York, USA
Importance Best-selling designer in the world

Raised in the Bronx by Jewish immigrant parents, Lauren initially worked as a salesman for a traditional menswear establishment called Brooks Brothers, and then for the tie-manufacturing firm of A. Rivetz & Co. He later opened his own necktie store, where he also sold ties of his own design under the label 'Polo'. In 1968, Lauren launched his Polo menswear range made up of smart shirts and suits aimed at professional males. Three years later he turned to tailored women's ready-to-wear fashions in fabrics such as Harris tweeds, silks and cashmere. In the 1980s, his 'lifestyle' branding extended to a range of home furnishings, from bed linen to furniture.

Following the Second World War, America became a leader in sportswear, influencing the growth of casual clothing around the world. New York City had been the centre of ready-to-wear manufacturing since the nineteenth century and American fashion emerged, not from couture salons, but from the garment factories located in Seventh Avenue. Lauren, like many others, is a

'I don't design clothes. I design dreams.'

product of this culture. He capitalised on the theme of 'classic good looks' – always appropriate and comfortably chic – by combining quality materials, excellent workmanship and attention to detail. His clothing created an image of country-club wealth. This appealed to his American clientele as their history was never linked to titled gentry or aristocratic privilege. Class status was instead based on money, expensive-looking clothing and accessories and a sense of inimitable good taste.

Lauren's costuming for the films *The Great Gatsby* (1973) and *Annie Hall* (1978) influenced the way millions dressed in the 1970s. In 1984 he transformed the Rhinelander Mansion into a flagship store for Polo Ralph Lauren. This venue was in keeping with the landed-gentry image of quality, tradition and prestige that had become associated with the Lauren brand.

In the 1990s Ralph Lauren began soliciting funds for charities through his Polo collection. Written across the windows of his stores, the text explains that a percentage of the money paid for goods will be donated to cancer care and prevention. It is a marketing technique that persuades buyers to enter his shops, supports a humanitarian cause and extends goodwill in the community.

Lauren, after receiving many awards, was inducted into the Coty Hall of Fame in 1986. In 1992, he received a Lifetime Achievement Award from the Council of American Fashion Designers and was elected Designer of the Year in 1996. In the mid-1990s, Lauren's company turned public and traded on the New York Stock Exchange under the symbol RL. By 1997, sales of $5 billion a year made him the best-selling designer in the world, and by 2007 he had 116 free-standing stores in the USA alone.

Calvin Klein

A master of branding, Calvin Klein's success was based on his quality products and exceptional marketing techniques. Heralded as America's Yves Saint Laurent, Klein designed for the American lifestyle; his clothes were simple, comfortable, light and easy to wear. One collection developed into the next, and the monochromatic and minimalist conservatism that underlined his garments secured the global appeal of his label. His clients included Jacqueline Onassis, Liv Ullmann, Lauren Hutton and Nancy Reagan.

Born 1942, New York, USA
Importance Brought exceptional marketing techniques to fashion

Like Ralph Lauren, Klein was raised in the Jewish immigrant community in the Bronx. He graduated in 1962 from the Fashion Institute of Technology and apprenticed with a cloak-and-suit manufacturer, Dan Millstein, for $75 per week. He sold his first samples to the department store Bonwit Teller, in 1967, and quickly moved into sportswear, combining linen blouses and flannel skirts.

Klein launched his own company in 1968, which later became Calvin Klein Inc. He acknowledges his greatest inspiration to Baron de Gunzburg, who was his mentor for many years and who introduced him to members of the elite fashion scene. Klein's first major showing, held at New York Fashion Week, was hailed a great success. His clothes were noted for their clean-cut and clearly defined lines, splendid fabrics and perfect, yet formless, cuts – all very characteristic of American 'purist' design.

It was in marketing that Klein's skills came to the fore, however. When advertising his designer jeans line, Klein promoted sexuality: quite literally, he sold tighter jeans than anyone else. 'Nothing comes between me and my Calvins', the slogan boasted. He used well-known American celebrity, Brooke Shields as the girl-next-door cover model to promote the range in a very sensual and provocative way. The campaign worked so well that he tried a similar approach with his underwear range. With the designer name branded onto the waistband, clearly visible above hipster trousers, they almost advertised themselves. When, in 1982, an enormous billboard advertised Klein's underwear in New York's Times Square, featuring Bruce Weber's seductive photography of muscular male bodies, it met well with the prevailing craze for health and fitness. The campaign was a brilliant success; branding had become big business in the 1980s.

'I make clothes people like to wear.'

In 2002, the conglomerate, Philips-Van Heusen (PVH) bought the company and, three years later, signed new licensing agreements for handbags, footwear and women's sportswear, which were to be distributed in Japan and Southeast Asia.

Tom Ford

Credited with the complete refashioning of Gucci – making it the 'hot' label of the 1990s – Tom Ford instigated the mania for employing new designers to reinvigorate established fashion houses. Within five years, Ford transformed the tired old status label of Gucci from a failing business into a $2.2 billion asset. Cited as the man responsible for dressing the final years of the twentieth century, *The New York Times* called him 'the ultimate fin de siécle designer'.

Born 1961, Texas, USA
Importance
Championed the rejuvenation of established fashion houses

Tom Ford began his career on Seventh Avenue, the heart of New York's rag trade. He always contended that he 'never pretended to be anything other than a commercial designer'. He worked briefly at Cathy Hardwick, Chloe and Perry Ellis before joining Gucci, in 1990, and he designed his first collection in 1994. A significant portion of Gucci's successful resurgence under Ford must be credited to his creating an 'aura'; one didn't just wear the clothes, one wore the lifestyle. Ford's sleek, sexy and sophisticated look for Gucci suited the international jet-set trend and was copied time and again by numerous high-street labels.

In terms of business, Ford takes a holistic approach; he becomes involved in advertising campaigns, store designs and the packaging. In design terms, he is a revivalist designer – he has featured looks from the 1960s,

'It's about celebrating… about hedonism, luxury, glamour and sex – I've always been in love with all those things.'

1970s and 1980s in his collections – and has promoted his fashion to the Asian market. Significantly, like many other contemporary fashion designers, almost half of his company's sales are in Asia.

Interestingly, while with Gucci, Ford collaborated with American performance artist Vanessa Beecroft to produce 'Show 2001' at New York's Guggenheim Museum. Models wearing Gucci designer swimwear stood immobilised, except for their gaze, as part of a large art installation. The publicity generated from this event brought international attention to the Gucci label.

When Gucci bought Yves Saint Laurent (YSL) in 2000, Ford also started designing the YSL ready-to-wear 'Rive Gauche' line. His first collection, in 2000, received a very lukewarm response but, by 2001, he seemed to have found his forte. By delving into the massive YSL archive, Ford borrowed exotic and gypsy romantic styles from Yves Saint Laurent's famous 'Carmen' collection to produce updated versions of the garments. When he left Gucci and Yves Saint Laurent in 2004, Ford worked freelance for Estée Lauder to reinvigorate some of its classic perfumes and, at the same time, started his own high-end menswear line, with a shop opening in 2007 on Madison Avenue in New York.

Tom Ford's latest menswear venture is best described as 'looking like Ford himself – matinee-idol handsome and sophisticated'. The clothes have an old-world glamour with a modern twist. Ford, like Karl Lagerfeld, is always immaculately dressed and exudes a confidence through his self-assured manner, which mirrors his success in the industry. It seems that he is a man who enjoys challenges, and has a unique ability to be a successful 'image-maker'.

MEN'S FASHION

In eighteenth-century France, during the reign of Louis XIV, men were referred to as the 'peacocks of fashion'. They wore very decorative Rhinegrave breeches covered in lace and bows made of the finest silks and satins; impeccably clean white linen shirts with lavish cravats; and overcoats called *justaucorps* adorned with lavish buttons and gold braid that stretched from chin to knee.

This form of conspicuous consumption was considered the epitome of good taste. After the French Revolution (1789), however, the canons of tasteful dress changed dramatically. Simplicity, starkness and refinement became the order of the day with long trousers, vests, frock coats and top hats defining the role of the gentleman in society. Well-tailored suits made from the finest cloth became the requisite of determining your position in society, and your delegation to the ranks of the upper classes. Tales of the infamous dandy, Beau Brummel, abound: a man who befriended the Prince of Wales in the early nineteenth century and set the benchmark for cleanliness and restraint in male attire, with understated but beautifully fitted and tailored clothing. He is credited with introducing and establishing the modern suit.

English male fashion, underlined by the British landed gentry, established the European stylistic trends of the nineteenth and early twentieth centuries. It was during this time that the tailors of London's Saville Row became famous for exquisitely cut and tailored garments for men. Saville Row was built between 1731 and 1735, originally as part of the Burlington Estate. Beau Brummel helped to establish its reputation as he patronised the tailors congregated on the Burlington Estate, who then started to occupy premises on Saville Row. Even contemporary designers, including John Galliano and

Alexander McQueen, chose to serve an apprenticeship in Saville Row, and no matter how outlandish their fashion garments appear, they retain respect and admiration for their industry through their masterful tailoring expertise.

In 1818, Harry Sands Brooks established Brooks Brothers, one of America's oldest retailers, known for its classic and conservative styling. It was the first company to offer ready-made suits to individuals like sailors, who were only on shore leave for a short time, and gold miners before they headed west. For over 100 years, they also supplied uniforms to the US military. The innovations of Brooks Brothers include the first summer seersucker suit (1830), suits and beachwear made from madras plaid (1890), the button-down collar shirt worn during polo matches (1896), Shetland wool sweaters (1904) and the first wash-and-wear Dacron and polyester shirts (1953). Always synonymous with fashionable, well-constructed garments, they attracted the business of celebrities such as the Rolling Stones and other pop stars of the 60s. The British company Marks and Spencer bought Brooks Brothers in 1988.

After the Second World War, the influence of American ready-to-wear had a worldwide impact on the direction of men's business suits and casual wear. Designers like as Ralph Lauren and Calvin Klein offered the ultimate in men's casual lifestyle dressing. Influenced by Italian designer, Giorgio Armani, and his informal, easy-fitting clothing, a new era in menswear was born. This loose-fitting styling was reinforced by menswear designed by the Japanese designers, Yohji Yamamoto and Rei and was adopted by new age, avant-garde males.

Miuccia Prada

Having become one of the world's leading designers out of circumstance rather than choice, Miuccia Prada is considered more eccentric and unconventional than many of her contemporaries. She enjoys creating a paradox in her work by combining opposites, whether that refers to stylistic oppositions or the placement of the old with the new, or careful and artful construction with spontaneous pastiche.

Born 1949, Milan, Italy
Importance Set trends that were emulated by other fashion houses

A highly educated woman with a doctorate in political science, Miuccia Prada inherited her grandfather's leather goods company in the mid 1970s. The Prada Company had been founded in 1913 by Mario Prada and was the luggage maker of choice to the Milanese aristocracy. Miuccia created the first nylon bag in 1978, and the classic simple, black nylon knapsacks with the silver-metal Prada label were presented in 1984. These became a cult item among fashion followers, and a style icon of the 1990s. The move inadvertently launched the craze for fashion labels to produce signature bags of their own.

Perhaps somewhat surprised by her initial success, Prada presented her first ready-to-wear collection in 1988. Considering her active commitment to political discussion and debate, it is not surprising that her design work was considered unconventional: it often embraced retro styling with offbeat colour and pattern combinations and made use of both high-tech and old-fashioned materials. Prada has, in various collections, combined stilettos with thick wool socks, fur helmets with cocktail dresses and tiaras

'I never actually decided to become a designer. Eventually, I found that I was one.'

with work clothes. She has described her designs variously as 'uniforms for the slightly disenfranchised' (the name given to her first collection) and as bad taste, 'I don't make elegant clothes anymore, but the opposite. I make ugly clothes from ugly material.' Techno styles make use of industrial materials and can express an industrial aesthetic, which in itself reflects cultural values. Prada's comment suggests that she is presenting buyers with a choice – a freedom to choose their own aesthetic. Her dresses decorated with celluloid strips defy convention, even her own conventions, thereby introducing an element of self-reflexivity into her design practice.

Prada's spirited and experimental fashions have a wide appeal in the twenty-first century, as they serve a purpose far greater than just adornment. Often drawing on the military uniform, like both Gucci and Dolce and Gabbana she exploits the erotic appeal of sartorial militarism. Guy Trebay, writing for *The New York Times,* in 2008, suggested that 'it is her engagement with mutating outlines of class that make her one of Italy's most compelling cultural exports'. An inadvertent trend setter, like Rei Kawakubo of Comme des Garçons, Prada commissioned Pritzker Prize awarded architects Rem Koolhaas to design the New York and Los Angeles flagship stores – called Prada Epicenter – which were opened in 2001 and 2004 resepctively, and Herzog and de Meuron to design another, in Tokyo, in 2003.

Dolce and Gabbana

Dolce and Gabbana clothing is known for its defiantly sexy and provocative styling. It exudes a vampish Italian 'sex-bomb' glamour typified by early 1950s screen sirens, such as Sophia Loren and Gina Lollabrigida. Their advertising campaigns are renowned for using provocative, sexy and edgy images.

Born (Domenico Dolce) 1958, Palermo, Sicily; (Stephano Gabbana) 1962, Venice, Italy
Importance
Reintroduced Italian glamour to fashion

Dolce and Gabbana (D&G) first showed their work under the banner of 'New Talent' at the Milan Collezioni in 1985. Their first women's collection, which was entitled 'Real Woman' (1986), has been described as post-feminist in the way that it allows women to reclaim stereotypical styles that would previously have been considered degrading. One of their biggest supporters, Madonna, who commissioned D&G to design 1,500 costumes for her 1993 'Girlie Show' world tour, is the epitome of this new image. It is a look based on empowerment and confidence, with a touch of irony.

D&G were among numerous designers who made underwear the accepted face of erotic display. Jean-Paul Gaultier, John Galliano and Vivienne Westwood have all used corsets as a theme for their collections. These garments, in which

'When we design, it's like a movie. We think of a story and we design the clothes to go with it.'

underwear becomes outerwear, explicitly provoke connotations of eroticism and challenge acceptable moral and gender codes. The satin corset became the new miniskirt, lingerie lookalike garments that were seductive and alluring and rhinestone-covered bodices became representative of the neo-glamorous image of the 1990s.

D&G opened their first boutique in Tokyo (1989), followed by Milan and Hong Kong, and finally London (1999). The D&G logo has become a worldwide symbol of a 'bling' and Italian sexiness, and many imitations exist. Always a favourite with Hollywood movie celebrities, fashion editors and a young moneyed party crowd, their clothes can be seen in all the fashionable clubs and bars of every major city. Their menswear collection also combines sexiness with classical elements. Pinstriped gangster-boss suits, printed and embroidered coats, and using black as the dominant colour became their trademarks. Yet they also produced a more casual collection; skilled Sicilian craftswomen and tailors produced casual, unstructured garments, coloured in earthy brown or black tones with a flash of scarlet. Leggings, instead of trousers, are coupled with tattoo-covered leather jackets, and knitted sweaters focus on surface textures.

Dolce and Gabanna are at the cutting edge of fashion, making beautiful and high-quality shoes, clothing and other products. Their work, which won the Woolmark award in 1991, appeals to both the straight and the gay community. They launched a lower-priced diffusion line in 1993. Today, perfume sales are instrumental to the success of leading fashion houses and their fragrance lines have also enjoyed great success, receiving a number of prestigious awards, including the International Prize of the Perfume Academy for best feminine fragrance of the year 1993; for best masculine fragrance in 1995; and the Oscar de Perfums Award for best men's fragrance in 1996; Best Men's fragrance for 'Light Blue Pour Homme', 2008; and the US Fifi award.

Alexander McQueen

Alexander McQueen is widely recognised as a highly innovative designer with superb tailoring skills. He apprenticed as a tailor with Saville Row's Anderson & Shepard and, from 1990 to 1992,

Born 1970, London, England

Importance Combined exquisite tailoring with avant-garde design

Gieves & Hawkes. While there, he mastered six methods of pattern cutting from the sixteenth century to the present day. It was this mastery that offered him opportunities to design for Gigli, Tatsuno, Givenchy and Gucci. He enrolled in a Masters' course at Central St Martin's School of Art and Design, which culminated in his 1992 'Jack the Ripper Stalking his Victims' collection. He was British Designer of the Year in 1996, 1997 and 2001.

McQueen launched his own line in 1992 and his collections have been characterised by outrageous imagery and performance. Notoriety followed him as he presented his 1994 'Nihilism' collection, his 1995 'The Birds' collection, and his 1996 'Highland Rape' collection, made up of tattered lace and models with dishevelled hair. His infamous, 1996 low-cut 'bumsters' revealed bottom cleavage, his 1997 *Bellmer la Poupée* collection featured models that looked like slaves wearing jewelled manacles, and his 1998 show highlighted the beauty of a disabled model with two false legs. In 1999, both models and dresses were sprayed with paint shooting from a mechanical device installed on the stage. McQueen's shows are slick, professional and sometimes aggressive visual spectacles, which are often held in traditionally working-class locations, such as Borough Market in London or an insane asylum. By contrasting

'The clothes I design are strong – they are meant to build confidence.'

glamorous outfits with a shabby, dirty environment, he heightens their appeal.

Designing for Givenchy in 1997, as well as for his own label, became a two-edged sword. The House of Givenchy was about elegance and beauty, and Alexander McQueen was about innovation, edgy design, and unique ideas. Yet McQueen was able to establish a signature style at the house of Givenchy before moving on to Gucci in 2000, when he sold 51 per cent of his own company to this label. Since 2002, his collection showings have become less riotous and more demure; he is concentrating more on the design of the clothes than the theatrics of the production. 'At some stage, you have to grow up. It's important now that people focus on the clothes rather than someone in a clown's suit', he said. In 2005, he held a retrospective show of his work over the years and showed Japanese kimonos, sci-fi bodysuits, moulded corsets and flounced skirts. When he designs for his own label, the work is charged with a personal emotionalism. In 2007, McQueen launched his McQ line intended for a younger, casual lifestyle, including jeans, T-shirts, miniskirts and knitwear.

John Galliano

At the graduating fashion show of London's Central St Martin's College of Art and Design in 1984, John Galliano's *Incroyables* collection was based on the clothing worn during the 'reign of terror' that followed the French Revolution of 1789. It took the audience by storm, and Joan Burstein of the prestigious Browns' boutique purchased all of the garments and placed them in her window. Galliano's future as a very exciting, cutting-edge fashion designer was secured.

Born 1961, Gibraltar
Importance Exposed the pure decadence of couture by 'turning it inside out'

As a student, Galliano made frequent visits to London's Victoria and Albert Museum, where he sketched and examined dresses made by Madeleine Vionnet, the master couture technician. He then worked for Tommy Nutter in Saville Row, where he experimented and further developed his skills in bias cutting and tailoring techniques. He opened a studio in Parsons' Green, London, in 1984, where he developed his reputation as an exciting cutting-edge designer. His work demonstrated a balance between fantasy and classicism, laced with historicism and extravagance. Like Yves Saint Laurent, Galliano's collections were diverse, ranging from the highlands of Scotland to sixteenth-century farthingale skirts, Japonism and 1940s gangster suits.

He was helped along the way by a number of influential people, namely Amanda Grieve (later Lady Harlech); Leon Tully, a creative director for American *Vogue*; John Bult, Swiss Chairman of Paine Webber International; Sao Schlumberger, who provided accommodation for him; and Bernard Arnault, president of Moët Hennessy-Louis Vuitton (LVMH). He was named British designer of the year in 1987, 1994, 1995 and 1997.

Arnault invited Galliano to become the head designer at Givenchy from 1995 to 1996 and, one year later, at Dior. While it seemed an unlikely choice at the time, one very consistent feature of Galliano's showings was the beauty and creativity of his garments. Romance is coupled with precision tailoring, which is particularly suited to the history of extravagant design at the House of Dior. He has been described by the fashion journalists as a 'boy wonder' and a 'romantic hero', but more recently, the reviews have commented that 'show, not clothes, become the message' with Galliano.

His fashion shows were billed as 'blockbusters' and were probably the most extravagant in Paris. Like theatrical stage productions, his collections were always themed and based on visual spectacle. In many cases, he transformed an existing venue to meet his fantasies: football stadiums were transformed into enchanted forests; the Paris Opera turned into an English tea party; and an old train station became an Eastern 'souk'. The audience not only viewed the garments on parade, but experienced the aura of the themed show. Galliano himself came dressed as if part of the charade, which made his showings seem more like a dress-up party than a marketing function.

Vivienne Westwood

British designer Vivienne Westwood pioneered fashion as sexual provocation, which she conveyed through her styling of garments, the stance of her models and the photographic portrayal of her work. Throughout the 1980s, her work, sometimes openly hostile to acceptable norms, drew great attention from the fashion press. Inspired by her lack of conformity, designers including Jean-Paul Gaultier, Zandra Rhodes, Thierry Mugler and Claude Montana also attempted to challenge the limits of acceptable fashion. It is not surprising that these trends paralleled the 1980s wave of feminist revolt.

Born 1941, Cheshire, England
Importance Imitated the eclectic punk look

Westwood became immersed in the 1970s punk era when she opened a boutique in London with Malcolm McLaren. They called the shop 'SEX'. In liaison with members of the Sex Pistols punk band, she imitated the punks' eclectic do-it-yourself look, which was meant to contradict all rules of high fashion. This highly aggressive and sometimes offensive approach to fashion design was to become her trademark throughout most of her career. She is particularly credited with producing innovative garments that turned underwear into outerwear, a trend that was copied by a number of other designers of the day.

While Westwood worked to sustain her anti-establishment reputation, she also consistently reinforced her ties to British fashion and her respect for historical costume techniques. In the 1990s, her collections revealed an interest in highly technical tailoring techniques and in the art of cutting. She studied the structure of historical costume at London's Victoria and Albert Museum and argued that 'to do anything original, you have to build on tradition'.

Her 'Pirate' collection of 1981 was unisex, and broke away from her use of black-on-black. It featured a jacket with slashes revealing bright orange patterned silk, worn by a young woman with rags tied in her hair. The collection was immediately embraced by

'In both political and social revolutions, the mode of dress worn becomes a badge of affiliation with the cause. The more committed a person is, the more evident it becomes in the dress.'

mainstream fashion. In 1987, classic garments included in the 'Harris Tweed' collection paid homage to the tailoring traditions of Saville Row and the heritage of British wool knits, gaberdines and tweeds. While Westwood's work parodied the English lifestyle, at the same time it helped to expand the export of British fabrics and other 'institutions' like Burberry. For this she was awarded the Queen's Award for Export Achievement in 1998, and later received an OBE from the queen. Westwood was named British Designer of the Year in 1990 and 1991. She has been one of Britain's most inventive and influential fashion designers. The themes for her collections have swung like a pendulum, from 'Anglomania' (1993) to 'Erotic Zones' and 'Vive La Cocotte' (1995) to 'Tied to the Mast' (1998) (inspired by Gericault's nineteenth-century painting *The Raft of the Medusa*). This type of contrast and contradiction is inherent to her work; it is historical yet, at the same time, has a timeless appeal.

WOMEN'S FASHIONS

Throughout history, women's dress signified their status and position in society through their ostentatious display of finery and excessive decoration. During the course of the late nineteenth and early twentieth centuries women's fashions transformed dramatically in response to changing social mores and attitudes.

At the turn of the century, the suffragettes protested for women's right to vote, own property and be educated, and they endorsed a more practical form of dress. They dared to wear garments without corsets, usually empire-waisted with many layers of soft, draped fabric. This 'reform dress', first introduced in the 1870s and 1880s, was endorsed by artists, feminist-minded women and rebellious youth. Frenchwoman, Herminie Cadolle started a revolution when she cut her corset in two in order to make it more comfortable. The upper part she called the *soutien gorge*, or breast support and it was displayed at the Universal exhibition of 1889 along with other engineering achievements of the day. In 1907, Vogue magazine first wrote of a new-fangled item of intimate apparel called the *brassiere*.

While bloomers had been worn under full dress by women described as having a 'wild spirit and radical socialist beliefs', trousers did not become part of an acceptable wardrobe until after the First World War. The designer Paul Poiret, in the 1910s, was one of the first of the early couturiers to produce sketches of women wearing trouser suits. Most of the significant changes in women's dress came from the practicalities of war. Women who worked in factories wore dungarees, and others wore masculine-looking uniforms while working as bus and tram operators.

When women gained the right to vote in the 1920s, they celebrated by wearing short skirts to the knees for the first time in history, as well as sleeveless bodices, V-necklines and razor-cut hairstyles. These new styles were all considered very risqué and often immoral. At this time, it is not surprising that Coco Chanel built a fashion empire with her practical and comfortable styled clothes that were initially inspired by menswear. Following the Second World War, Christian Dior responded to the psychological need to feminise fashion again and introduced his 'New Look' collection which returned the hourglass silhouette, the demure 'off the shoulder' neckline and the full billowing skirts.

By the late 1960s however, when the Women's Emancipation League demanded equal pay for equal work, many women (and men), as a sign of solidarity, adopted unisex outfits, and many wore 'bra-less' see-through blouses and miniskirts. This blatant exposure of the female body was meant to shock and break down the sexual taboos of the past. When sex equality legislation was finally passed by many Western countries in the 1980s, another wave of independent dressing trends appeared in the form of power dressing. Masculine shoulder-padded jackets created a no-nonsense executive look and designers including Jean Paul Gaultier, Thierry Mugler and Gianni Versace showed collections with models wearing revealing super-chic tight black leather outfits resplendent with chains and fringing. In 1990, Gaultier designed the cone brassiere for Madonna's 'Blonde Ambition' tour, making this piece of apparel a cultural icon.

The past 20 years have seen a trend in dressing that highlights individual needs, rather than collective styling. Mix-and-match dressing, ethnic-inspired clothing, the grunge look, street style styling or the wearing of vintage dress allowed women to reveal their own personalities and to embrace meaning and memory in their choice of clothing. The appropriation of retro dress, in particular, responded to the growing influence of the film and multi-media industry, a form of popular culture that has had a significant impact upon society.

Yohji Yamamoto

With a career spanning three decades, Yohji Yamamoto has consistently challenged existing conventions in fashion, building a career on proving that black is beautiful. He has a craftsman's sense of materials, starting every collection with the fabric and then letting the collection take its shape. Because his clothes deconstruct, they are termed anti-fashion, yet he insists that clothes must be used to evoke an emotional response and that they must be linked with the everyday.

Born 1943, Tokyo, Japan
Importance Created great dignity in fashion through the deconstruction of form

Along with Rei Kawakubo, Yamamoto paraded black, ripped and torn, shroud-like garments on the catwalks of Paris in 1983, shocking the international fashion industry. Journalists called the collection a revolution in twentieth-century fashion, where a 'look of poverty' rather than one of glamour, was being celebrated. The models' bodies were wrapped with layer after layer of dark fabric, giving the impression of clothing that was unfinished, with uneven and unstitched hemlines and oddly positioned pockets and fastenings. In defence of their work, the designers insisted that there was great dignity and beauty in the clothing and that it symbolised the hardships and oppression that so many people have had to bear in their lives.

Growing up in post-war Tokyo under the supervision of his

dressmaking mother, Yamamoto decided to study fashion design. Having already graduated from law school, Yamamoto attended the Bunka Fashion College in Tokyo from 1966 to 1968. A major theme in his work is based on a duality of identity – clothing that is neither Eastern nor Western, male nor female, non-revealing yet seductive. He remarked that 'When I first started designing, I wanted to make men's clothes for women. But there were no buyers for it. Now there are…I think that my men's clothing look as good on women as my women's clothing (does)'.

Yamamoto has great expertise in tailoring, and was instrumental in changing the look of the traditional Western man's business suit. By removing the linings and shoulder padding, eliminating the curved seaming in the jacket, and widening the trousers, the heavy, structured garment became much lighter, more relaxed and comfortable. His wit and humour was reflected in the details of his garments – the permanently creased collars, the contrasting colour of the threads that he made visible on the surface of the garments, and the long threads or tendrils that hung down from the cloth in conspicuous areas. In the 1990s, he popularised the combination of wearing a black suit over a white T-shirt.

'Black is modest and arrogant at the same time'

In the 1990s, Yamamoto presented multifaceted collections where the influence of Victorian crinolines and Edwardian bustles dominated. He paid homage to a number of the great Western designers including Coco Chanel, Christian Dior and Yves Saint Laurent. By imitating their styling, he proved to the world that his handling of fabric, his ability to cut, construct and define silhouette was equal to the best of the haute couture world.

Rei Kawakubo

Rei Kawakubo has collaborated extensively with other visual practitioners to extend the boundaries of what constitutes fashion in today's society by reconsidering the role of status, display and sexuality. As a result, her clothing is the ultimate in postmodern avant-garde design: it references past traditions; it challenges the notion of haute couture both as an elitist activity and in terms of its flawless construction techniques; and it offers a social or political critique of society.

Born 1942, Tokyo, Japan
Importance
Intellectualised fashion using unconventional methods and materials

Kawakubo is the founder of Comme des Garçons. Approaching design from a totally conceptual perspective, she finds beauty in the unfinished, the irregular, the monochromatic and the ambiguous. She takes an intellectual approach and works with ideas as much as fabric. Like Yohji Yamamoto, her designs reflect a 'deconstructivist' approach, where refurbished garments are repeatedly slashed, spoiled, knotted and distressed – the opposite of constructing a garment.

In the 1980s, Kawakubo used black, as it assumed the status of a non-colour; it becomes an absence rather than a presence. Her trademark use of asymmetrical lines, texture and sculptural layering underlines each of her collection shows. Like Madeleine Vionnet, the complexity of the pattern pieces suggests that they must be unpicked to understand how they fit together. The irregularity of the construction of the garments is appreciated when looking at these flat, abstracted pieces. In her 1983 Spring/Summer Collection, she featured a beige calico skirt and top that epitomised the social uncertainties that marked this era, symbolised by the flaws that appeared as an inherent aspect of her textile design: holes in the design added dimension to the fabric, allowing the layering below to show through. Kawakubo's leading textile designer, Hiroshi Matsushita, devised the technique – referred to as 'loom-distressed weaves' – by reformulating the fabric on the loom. Kawakubo's 'lace' knitwear, as it was called, demonstrated how her garments were purposely knitted to incorporate various sized holes that appear as rips and tears. Kawakubo found beauty in the irregularity of the weave. These garments were worn with leggings of surgical elasticised bandage and wrap-over deerskin bootees.

'Not what has been seen before, not what has been repeated, instead new discoveries that look to the future.'

Comme des Garçons philosophy

The 'Bump' collection of 1997 provoked another reactionary response. Here, Kawakubo shattered all traditions by totally distorting the human figure in grotesque proportions by adding padding in the most unexpected places – over the abdomen, between the shoulder and the breast and in the middle of the back. Fashion writers presumed she was making a feminist statement about how fashion can undermine the sexuality of the female figure. Kawakubo does not explain her intentions, as she believes that the clothing should speak for itself.

Contemporary Avant-garde

Franco Moschino

With roots in the surrealist revival that occurred during the late 1980s, Franco Moschino's fashion was all about satire and irony. He loved the surreal impact of Magritte's painting and used the surrealist technique of displacement – placing incongruous images side-by-side in order to create an impact. His clothing made a social statement and like Elsa Schiaparelli, wit and humour were part of the message.

Born 1950, Lombardy, Italy
Importance Parodied fashion, criticising the materialistic nature of the industry
Died 1994, Milan, Italy

Moschino first studied art at the Accademia delle Belle Arti, in Milan, from 1968 to 1971, but soon turned to tailoring and fabrics as his preferred tools of trade. He worked as a freelance designer and illustrator and briefly sketched for Versace. In 1977, Moschino became a designer for the Italian company Cadette, starting his first company Moonshadow and launching Moschino 'Couture!' in 1983.

Moschino made bodices out of safety pins, a scorch-mark-printed silk shirt saying 'too much ironing', and a winter coat of stitched-together teddy bear pelts. He adopted a 1960s neo-pop approach in creating his anti-fashion statements, which were not just directed against the materialism of the industry but towards the buyers as the fashion victims as well. His facetious Rolex necklace, seemingly made from recycled watch parts, commented on a brand name associated with wealth, and his garments made from mixing cheap plastics with expensive fur were methods that he used to give his fashion products meaning. He introduced his diffusion line, 'Cheap and Chic', in 1988, which was chic but not necessarily cheap. His parody of fashion continued in 1990 with an 'Organic Bikini'

'Fashion should be fun and should send a message.'

made by sowing and watering real grass, hats in the form of wedding cakes and white handbags appearing to drip with melted chocolate. His 'Label Queen Dress', made from shopping bags for a window display in his New York boutique on Madison Avenue, typified his critical comments about the levels of consumerism in society.

This type of fun imagery, borrowed from film, animation, media and pop culture made his fashion goods even more popular. Consumers didn't seem to mind that he was mocking them and trying to destabilise the fashion system. In Dadaist style, he hurled abuse at the system, its clients and the fashion press alike and received their applause in return. The irony, however, was that this type of reflexive critique was making his business financially stronger.

Moschino's visual gags and jokey logos were further enhanced by his fashion shows, which were more akin to performance art, underlined by an element of unpredictability. In his couture show, he pumped up jackets and stoles made from inflatable PVC materials. His 1994 'Ecoculture' collection, launched on the Nature Friendly label, was the first high fashion clothing designed using environmental-friendly materials and dyes. He presented a sexy black evening gown worn with a clear plastic fitted jacket with white stitching and text running across the back which stated 'Ecology now? Ecology wow!'

Well ahead of other designers, Moschino embraced technology, using short videos to highlight a selection of the clothes in his collection. After his death, a foundation was established in his name to help children battling HIV and AIDS and his firm routinely designed for charities and fundraisers such as Artwalk New York.

Ann Demeulemeester

Ann Demeulemeester made her name by 'opposing and even mocking the barbarism' of the 1990s. Her very serious and quietly intense clothing is known for its experimental cuts and use of atypical fabrics including paper, leather, painter's canvas and distressed suede. Fabrics are often cut asymmetrically, wrapped, draped or twisted and occasionally come with instructions on how to wear them. She describes her clothes as romantic, poetic, elaborate and wild.

Born 1959, Kortrijk, Belgium
Importance Pioneered deconstructivism in fashion

Ann Demeulemeester graduated from the Antwerp Academy of Fine Art in 1981, produced her first women's collection in 1987 and a men's collection in 2005. Her design philosophy, like that of the other members of the 'Belgian Six' (Martin Margiela, Dries Van Noten, Marina Yee and Dirk Bikkembergs), follows the deconstructivist ideas of French philosopher Jacques Derrida whose writings have influenced fashion, film, design and architecture.

The Belgian Six came to prominence in avant-garde fashion in the 1980s, representing a new generation of young designers. Drawing on 1970s styling and early 1980s Japanese designer collections, they spearheaded a new direction in European fashion, which was called

'I'm not confused about what's happening in fashion, because I follow my own direction and go.'

'deconstruction'. In fashion design, deconstruction relates to using techniques in which the asymmetrical cuts dominate, seams and fasteners are highlighted, openings appear in unusual places and edges are frayed and unfinished. The clothes often have uneven hemlines, are either oversized or shrunken, and are generally black.

Demeulemeester's garments cleverly appear to be slipping off the body and are held together by an internal harness system. She has also made garments from modules or sections that can be added or taken away. Ideas normally associated with traditional fashion, such as clothing that enhances the figure, or makes the wearer appear to be more beautiful, are also negated or 'deconstructed'. In other words, importance is placed on the process of creation – whether conceptual or technical – and the end product is secondary. Her work has often been compared to early Rei Kawakubo and Yohji Yamamoto for its conceptual base, unstructured appearance and monochromatic palette in black, white or grey. This 'distressed' look in international fashion was often discussed in relation to the economic recession suffered in the early 1980s and was seen as fashion's response to global conditions.

Demeulemeester has often collaborated with artists and musicians, including Jim Dine for her 1999 asymmetrically-cut dresses with patterns made from silver-grey photos of birds of prey and Steven Klein for her 2004 'Horses' collection. The latter, highly acclaimed collection was inspired entirely by horses and included, among other items, trousers that looked like jodhpurs, except that the side volume was made by removable pockets, and a transformable riding coat whose buttons were replaced by straps and could be adapted for use as a jacket, coat or skirt. Her work has been included in a number of key exhibitions including 'Wild: Fashion Untamed' (2005), 'Goddess' (2003) at the Metropolitan Museum of Art, New York and the 1996 Biennale of Florence.

FABRIC TECHNOLOGY

Historically, the fashion industry has been built on the textile industry with Paris as the centre of haute couture, in part, owing to its silk manufacturing history. Subsequently, the nineteenth-century search for a synthetic substitute for natural raw materials centred on finding an 'artificial silk' that was durable and inexpensive.

In 1884, Count Chardonnet patented the process for preparing and dissolving nitrocellulose in such a way that it could be forced through a jet. Despite the fact that the process was quite hazardous, causing alarming explosions, fabrics made from the silk-like filaments were called 'rayon' and placed on display at the Artificial Silk Exhibition of 1926, in London. By 1938, nylon was commercially produced by Du Pont in the United States and in 1940 women could purchase their first nylon stockings. By 1966, over a third of all fabrics were synthetic and were no longer considered the cheap alternatives to luxury fabrics. In the late 1960s, American scientists developed a textile called Kevlar. A man-made, organic, bulletproof fibre (still used in bulletproof vests), it had high strength, high cut resistance and high chemical (including fire and water) resistance. It has been incorporated into motorcyclist riding gear such as jeans and jackets.

Hybrid engineered textiles can be part textile and part non-textile – perhaps incorporating glass, metal, carbon and ceramic. Alexander McQueen's Spring/Summer 1996 collection used a synthetic fabric that was spattered with stainless steel. Fabric finishing using heat set provides protection for many textiles such as Tyvek. Designer Hussein Chalayan used this type of non-woven industrial fabric in a dress that resembled synthetic paper, and which was washable, durable and resistant to chemicals. Jean-Paul Gaultier used the dramatic effects of computer-generated imagery on fabrics with reactive dyes for his Spring/Summer 1996 collection. Chemical reactive dyes can produce more vibrant and finer detailed prints than was previously possible. A Japanese company called Omikenshi is developing a new type of viscose yarn called Crabyon made from crab shells which, when combined with cotton, kills 90 per cent of known bacteria that might attack the material.

Most recently, the Innovation Centre at Central St Martin's School of Art and Design is investigating the possibilities of multisensory design in making responsive clothing that changes with emotion. Specifically, research is looking into the impact of 'aromochology', where fragrance is incorporated in a fabric to enhance one's sense of well-being and emotional stability. Other 'smart' textiles include fabrics encapsulating 'phase change materials' (PCM), which absorb heat energy when they change from a solid to a liquid state and release heat energy when they revert back. This has a temporary cooling or heating effect on the clothing layer, thereby keeping the wearer comfortable. 'Thermo chromic materials' (TCM) sense changes in the environmental temperature, which accordingly changes the colour of the fabric to suit the external climate.

Wearable technology involves the incorporation of external devices into clothing, which act as a prosthetic enhancement in some way. Companies such as Philips have been involved in combining fashion design with their personal audio devices and other technology for many years, such as sports clothing with built-in satellite navigation, headphones and heart rate monitors. More global electronic corporations will be working with artists and designers in the future to capitalise on potential emerging technologies.

Martin Margiela

Inspired by the notion of deconstruction, Martin Margiela 'uses clothes to critique clothes'. While his tailoring can be exquisite, his clothing exposes seams that highlight the fabrication process. Linings are revealed, and sometimes reversed, showing the seams on the outside, and frayed edges. Loose threads hang down like tentacles, and the fabric texture draws your attention to surface renderings.

Born 1957, Louvain, Belgium
Importance Used deconstructivist methods to challenge the conventions of fashion

Trained at the Royal academy of Fine Arts in Antwerp, Margiela was a member of the group known as the 'Belgian Six'. He moved to Paris in 1982 and worked for Jean-Paul Gaultier for five years. He then founded a company with Jenny Meirens and, in 1988, they presented their first women's ready-to-wear collection in Paris. The next year Margiela opened his own salon. His first collection featured models walking down a length of white fabric wearing socks saturated in red paint, leaving red footprints.

In the early 1990s, Margiela recycled garments and fabrics, using them to make something new or different: 1950s ball gowns were overdyed in grey and worn with old jeans; aprons and tops were made from old headscarves; stage costumes were transformed; and garments from the 1940s were cut up and reconstituted. This form of anti-aesthetic extends to Margiela's use of unorthodox materials, such as dresses made from plastic bags and sticky tape, and to construction methods where shoulder pads are pinned to the outside of the garments.

'Clothing is designed to be worn. When it is worn it is seen by people up close. This is not the case with the catwalk. It is not seen in the same quarters as in life.'

Classified as a 'deconstructivist', Margiela, in his search for greater intellectual credibility in fashion, forces the viewer to question existing conventions relating to fashion. His Spring/Summer 2000 collection, called 'Size 74', featured ridiculously oversized coats, shirts, lingerie and men's business shirts. The garments dwarfed the wearers, making them look quite ridiculous. Seen on coat hangers, viewers must adjust their focus to imagine what their clothes would look like in a normal size range. They instinctively question the notion of model's sizing – usually size 6 or 8 – as opposed to a normal woman's size and, in turn, ask what is considered 'average'. This clever contradiction plays havoc with a crucial concern of contemporary fashion.

Like many other contemporary designers, Margiela uses theatrical devices to enhance his collection showings. Collections have been organised like treasure hunts, where journalists are given maps of Paris and must find where the models will be parading the next section of the show. Video tapes are recorded leaning on one side so that the viewer, when playing the tape back, must turn the monitor on its side. Margiela's work was exhibited in 1997 in Rotterdam and again the same year with Rei Kawakubo. He worked as a very successful designer for Hermès from 1997 until 2004, when Jean-Paul Gaultier took over.

Issey Miyake

Issey Miyake has been dubbed the 'Picasso of fashion', but he does not want to be called an artist. Since his first collection was shown on the catwalks of Paris in 1973, he has inspired a generation of designers and design students alike. He has challenged the shape of fashion, the role that function and aesthetics play in today's fashion world, and has rejuvenated modern methods of clothing production.

Born 1935, Hiroshima, Japan
Importance Created sculptural forms that turned fashion into art

Miyake draws on the past, the present and the future in his work, coupling his Japanese heritage with challenging new technologies. The Japanese textile industry has become renowned for its cutting-edge fabrics and Miyake has worked in collaboration with textile designers for over 30 years, developing fabrics that are 'as fine as a butterfly's wings' or that can be heat-pleated to form zigzag patterns on the surface of the cloth.

First introduced in 1993, his 'Pleats, Please' range – which remains unequalled by any other designer trying to capture the same lightness and flexibility – is now fashioned from cloth that has been cut by using ultrasonic waves that emit heat vibrations. Miyake has gone to great lengths to illustrate his production techniques by means of a series of drawings on his website. They inform potential customers about the complexity in making a garment. He has also worked collaboratively with other artists, such as Yasuma Morimura, who place their images on the surface of the fabric before it is finely pleated, adding a new dimension to the artist's original work. This 'pleats and polyester' series of clothing, for

'I feel that I have found a new way to give individuality to today's mass-produced clothing.'

which Miyake is most famous, has been displayed in major art museums and galleries around the world including Tokyo, San Francisco, London, Paris and Amsterdam.

Miyake's clothes celebrate the vitality of the human body, which explains why he shows his clothes in movement. Miyake's inspiration has long been the spirit of the Japanese kimono; he believes that it is the space between the body and the cloth that creates a natural freedom. A major retrospective exhibition of his work was held in 1998 at the Cartier Foundation for Contemporary Art in Paris, where the garments were described as looking like swaying party lanterns, exotic birds flapping their wings or gaily coloured parachutes floating to the ground.

Miyake's next major range, entitled 'A-POC' (A Piece of Cloth), introduced in 1998, responded to his need to create a new form of clothing production where the garments were cut from large tubes of material, so minimising waste. Presented to the public as an art performance, he explains that these one-size-fits-all garments can be worn in any way the customer wishes. Miyake feels that 'people should participate in their own clothing'. He also sees this revolutionary range as a type of universal dress that could be sent to different places – Africa, the Middle East – and that it could be the future of fashion. Both the Pleats, Please and A-POC ranges are heralded as icons in the fashion world as they represent an attempt to redefine the role of design in daily life.

Viktor & Rolf

Referred to as the 'kings' of the international avant-garde fashion scene, Viktor & Rolf emerged at a time when haute couture was floundering. Revivalist fashions had been in full swing for 20 years and it seemed that, by the 1990s, they had nowhere to go. Journalists and design houses alike were forecasting the fall of the haute couture industry. Recognising this dilemma, in 1992, Viktor & Rolf adopted a post-war Dadaist approach in their critique of high fashion, challenging existing traditions and trends, and dared to treat haute couture in a humorous way.

Born (Viktor Horsting) 1969, the Netherlands; (Rolf Snoeren) 1969, the Netherlarnds
Importance Mocked haute couture traditions with their Dadaist approach to design

Two graduate art students of the Academia of Arnhem, Viktor & Rolf showed their first collection in 1998. The collection become a type pf 'performance art' as on the catwalk they depicted a model placing a new garment over the one that she was already parading for the audience. A dresser appeared on stage to help her place layer upon layer of garments on her body until her small frame became voluminous. This catwalk display critiqued the notion that 'thinner was better' and evoked such hilarity from the audience that it turned the seriousness of the occasion into a comedy. Like Elsa Schiaparelli, 60 years earlier, the satirical collection was well covered in the press but Viktor & Rolf sold next to nothing.

They continued to sensationalise high fashion in numerous collections, with distorted figures and exaggerated forms, often riddled with deliberate mistakes and contradictions. They parodied the Japanese designers by presenting all-black garments on black-painted models, and they irreverently suggested that fashion could be bigger than life. Their collection showings continued to be art performances in which the body was presented as a non-sexual and non-gendered object. Viktor & Rolf ridiculed haute couture as pretentious theatre where the pompous creations could not be worn in real life, but were designed for the stage only.

As part of their 2000 Autumn/Winter collection, Viktor & Rolf continued to parody this notion of 'fashion-as-spectacle' when they designed clothing – evening coats and tuxedo jackets – that were covered in small gold and silver balls. The visual pun implied was that this was 'fashion with bells on'. It was a form of anti-fashion, a self-reflective critique of the industry. In another outrageous collection, they didn't show any clothes at all, only placards painted with the words 'V & R are on strike'. When they were financially broke, Viktor & Rolf held an art installation, instead of a fashion parade, that was comprised of press clippings about themselves. This earned them a toungue-in-cheek recognition for being 'conceptual' fashion designers.

Their 2000/2001 collection was their greatest triumph: their first ready-to-wear 'Stars and Stripes' collection. While on the one hand, they seemed to mock American nationalism, on the other, they presented red, white and blue garments that the Americans would buy, including sweatshirts, polo necks and jeans. This kicked off their first commercially successful mass-produced range of clothing. A retrospective exhibition of the work of Viktor & Rolf was held in the Decorative Arts Museum of the Louvre in October 2003 to correspond to the 2003/2004 Spring/Summer prêt-à-porter collection showings.

Jun Takahashi

Emerging from a Tokyo street style background, Takahashi's cult street fashion brand is taking both America and Europe by storm. As Japan's newest fashion star, Takahashi's clothes offer the wearer multiple options, as they can be turned inside out to create an entirely different outfit and look. This 'metamorphosis' has captured the imagination of Japanese consumers, and Takahashi's 1994 label, Undercover, has been so popular that he now has over 30 retail outlets in Japan.

Born 1969, Kiryu, Japan
Importance Presented playful clothes where the shapes and silhouettes could be changed freely

Taken under Rei Kawakubo's wing, Takahashi went to Paris in 1998 with his 'Exchange' collection, which he presented in the prestigious Paris Colette store. His 1999 'Ambivalence' collection presented reversible clothing that was worn on the catwalk by twins, each wearing a different side. These novel clothes were versatile and fun, creating a paradox similar to those of surrealist artists: a casual denim jacket turned into an elegant fur dress; a second denim jacket turned into a nylon windbreaker.

Having graduated from the Bunka Academy of Fashion in 1991, Takahashi opened his first store in 1993 called Nowhere, featuring stuffed animals that had been torn apart and remade, displayed in a glass showcase. He participated in Tokyo Fashion Week in 1995 and made his Paris debut in the Spring/Summer 2003 collection. His collection, made up of appliqué trousers, was described as 'a work of art'. In his 'Witch's Cell Division' theme of the same year, items were disassembled through fasteners and reassembled in different combinations. The models faces, bodies and clothing were decorated with black etchings, like tattoos, made up of moons, stars and witchery images. This unique, playful, collection was a mix of a loose street aesthetic with dressier styles, with slightly strange and humorous results.

In a collection dedicated to Czech visual artist Jan Svankmajer, and his film, *Alice* (1988), which portrayed Alice (in Wonderland) in a decaying environment, Takahashi created Edwardian dresses made of silk with lace and tulle decoration that appeared to be rotting and falling apart. Details included embroidered trim that resembled decayed teeth and buttons shaped like eyeballs. This eclectic use of colour and pattern and the layering of cloth has become a key characteristic of Takahashi's work.

Not only is Takahashi's work politically inspired – he often writes text slogans on his T-shirts that deal with world issues – but elements of surreal romanticism surface consistently, showing a dark side to the beautiful creations that he produces. His Autumn/Winter 2006/07 collection showed models with their faces completely covered, like prisoners with bags placed on their heads before execution. His latest collections border on the mysterious, the fantastic, almost appearing to reveal some kind of inner psychological feeling or disturbance. Like most Harajuku fashion, Takahashi's work is influenced greatly by the media, anime and manga.

FASHION PHOTOGRAPHY

At the turn of the twentieth century, fashion houses favoured pedestrian photographs of their clothing. One of the earliest commercial photographic agencies, Seeberger Frères of Paris, documented the fashion in a true and factual manner, recording an exact reproduction of the garments usually set within a grandiose interior space. Props were also used, such as sheaves or baskets of flowers, period furniture, tapestries, paintings or satin pillows and ostrich fans.

This tradition of artificial decor persisted well into the century and was epitomised in the work of Baron de Meyer. His skilful use of backlighting, coupled with a soft focus, gave his sitters an ethereal beauty. He was able to persuade ladies of British aristocracy to sit for his fashion portraits, which, with their approval, were sold publicly later. Edward Steichen, who initially imitated de Meyer's cosmetic techniques, was the first to photograph a live model for a 1913 *Vogue* publication. He gradually moved away from the 'posed' silhouette and attempted to capture a more life like shot using natural light sources. The very serious and haughty facial expressions of his 1911 photos of Paul Poiret's models foreshadowed the 'look' that became synonymous with elegance in later catwalk shows.

Modernist photographers such as Horst P. Horst created the more dramatic and glamorous shots of the 1930s by using contrasting lighting techniques that created rich, dark areas of shadow. George Hoyningen-Huené used clear, bright lighting techniques in which the models became more inanimate, almost imitating the mannequins that appeared frequently in surrealist paintings. Alex Brodovitch, editor of *Harper's Bazaar* from the late 1940s to the early 1960s, encouraged photographers such as Richard Avedon and Irving Penn to use their photography as a means of creative expression. The architectural elements in the designs of Cristóbal Balenciaga led Penn to use empty backgrounds to create dramatic yet elegant forms that represented sculpture more than dress. Avedon engaged with the vitality of his subjects and the times; subsequently, using the narrative 'to tell the story' became fundamental in the construction of his fashion images. Composed studio photography disappeared in favour of more spontaneous exterior shots.

With the 1960s emphasis on youth and movement, fashion photography became much more dynamic. David Bailey used fragments of fashion and turned his subjects on the diagonal to give energy to his compositions. Outrageous fashion shots followed, with models photographed floating down the Seine River in plastic bubbles and being dropped from helicopters into haystacks. Later in the decade, a mood of decadence prevailed, with Helmut Newton infusing his work with pornographic connotations. His 'lurid look' became his trademark and was accepted for publication in Paris, but not in Britain or America.

The idea of marketing the product image rather than the product itself was taken to new heights with innovators such as Newton and Guy Bourdin in the 1970s. In Bourdin's campaigns for Charles Jourdan, the image is no longer one of playful sensuality but one of sex and death. His photographs take on the new dimension of social commentary with themes of tragedy and provocation. Both Nick Knight and David LaChapelle are technical innovators. Their work is not about representing fashion, but rather 'about the concept of fashion'. Knight insisted that fashion shoots were performances, and that the Internet allowed catwalk collections to enter the global home entertainment arena. His website covers both art and fashion and is renowned for its experimental interactive projects.

Levi Strauss

Levi jeans have achieved iconic status in the history of American fashion. Like Coca Cola, they were cleverly marketed as 'the real deal' – authentic, original and dependable. Levi Strauss and Company spans five generations and has remained privately owned. As one of the world's largest manufacturers of men's, women's and children's jeans and sportswear, it employs over 30,000 people worldwide.

Born 1829, Bavaria, Germany
Importance Introduced jeans to the world
Died 1902, California, USA

Originally, Levis Strauss formed a partnership with a tailor, Jacob Davis, who had developed a pair of trousers that had rivet metal at the stress points on the pockets and fly. In 1873, they patented the first Levi waist overalls. Jean cloth evolved as a cotton-based material that was used for very durable work clothes that did not chafe or wear out easily. With the 1848 gold rush in California, gold miners needed clothing that was strong and sturdy and they purchased these denim waist overalls from Strauss's dry-goods store.

The brand became distinctive in 1886, with double-stitched pockets, rivets and a large, leather two-horse label. In 1936 a red tag was attached to the back left pocket in order to identify the Levi's 501 brand at a distance. When American soldiers wore Levi's jeans overseas during the Second World War, the product's reputation gained international momentum.

In the 1950s, sales continued to skyrocket as the jeans were indirectly popularised by Hollywood western movies – which dominated the silver screen – and the newly invented television. Actors like Gene Autry and Roy Rogers became the heroes of the 'wild west'. In this post-war period, with social attitudes changing, jeans became a symbol of youthful revolt, immortalised in movies such as *The Wild One* (1953) featuring Marlon Brando and *Rebel Without a Cause* (1955) starring James Dean. Middle-class teenagers adopted denim jeans, overalls and jackets in the 1960s, as they epitomised the anti-establishment sentiment embraced by the hippie movement. Levi's appeared in their very first television commercial in 1966 and they expanded into women's apparel in 1968 to correspond with the Women's Liberation Movement. In 1971, the firm was awarded the Coty Fashion Critic's Award, America's most prestigious fashion trophy.

By the 1980s, jeans had been adopted as designer wear and the competition in the industry became fierce. Levi's was not able to compete with the trendier designer lines, which considered new options and were marketed differently. Branding competition saw firms such as Calvin Klein capitalise on the designer's name as a status symbol, and new systems of distribution emerged where private label lines were sold through department stores such as J. C. Penny's, Sears and Macy's in America. Jeans took on new identities as they targeted youth groups such as rap dancers, skateboarders and the like.

As the styling of the original Levi's had changed little, and the firm did not recognise the advantages of marketing and selling online, sales began to decline. The market was flooded with cheap mass-produced versions as international trade regulations were weak, and offshore manufacturing was increasing at an alarming rate. Yet the Levi Strauss firm was able to stand firm and adopted new marketing strategies to secure their place in the market. By 1992, over 450 million jeans, across all manufactured brands had been sold for a total sum of $8.2 billion and becoming one of the most successfully marketed clothing items in history.

Alfred Cartier

An exhibition held at the British Museum in February 1998, celebrated the work of Cartier from 1900 to 1939. Exquisite small, well-formed necklaces encrusted with diamonds and emeralds, sophisticated cigarette holders and cases, compact and detailed watches and solid, engraved and enamelled gold visiting card envelopes appeared in a myriad of forms. With influences from Egypt, Persia, India and the Russian tsars, the exhibition was a clear demonstration of the firm's skill for some of the most covetable jewellery the world has ever seen.

Born 1841, Paris, France
Importance Created jewellery of exquisite quality
Died 1925, France

Over the centuries, Cartier has made its name as an exclusive jewellery workshop and gained a fine reputation for well-crafted and high-quality goods. A family business, Cartier Jewellers dates back to 1847, when Louis-Francois sold jewellery and art objects in a number of Paris shops. In 1899, his son, Alfred, and grandson, Louis, opened the famous shop at 13 rue de la Paix, at the centre of the haute couture and jewellery district. A London branch was opened in response to the overwhelming number of commissions received to create custom pieces in commemoration of Edward VII's coronation, in 1902. The last of the three grand stores was opened in New York, in 1909, by his grandson Pierre.

Jewels originating from the great houses, such as Cartier, were usually designed anonymously. However,

'the jeweller of Kings, the King among jewellers'

Edward VII

in 1919, illustrator Georges Barbier, designed a collection of jewellery for Cartier, which consisted of anklets of pearls linked to bracelets, breastplates of pearls and a helmet. Fantasy and elaboration went hand-in-hand with elaborate evening dresses in the interwar years. Cartier introduced platinum or white gold to fine jewellery, as it exhibited great strength in the finest settings.

The firm exhibited its work at the International Exposition of Modern Industrial and Decorative Arts in Paris in 1925. In keeping with the period colours, Cartier displayed brilliant contrasts of emeralds with rubies, sapphires or turquoises. The *broche de décolleté* was an innovatory dress clip or clasp introduced at the exhibition, along with diamond curls that clipped to the hair or eyebrow, and convertible jewels that served dual purposes – a brooch, for example, that turns into a pendant. A double clip was composed of two interlocking sections that could be worn separately or as a single piece. Diamonds were often mixed with coloured gemstones to give the pieces more variety and contrast, and baguette cuts became increasingly popular for outlines and borders. Geometric form became very pronounced during the 1930s, but Cartier turned to floral patterns near the end of the decade.

Cartier was a large commercial house, renowned more for its workmanship than for cutting-edge design. Jewellery design was suspended for a six-year period during the Second World War. Between 1945 and 1962, Cartier's chief designer, Jeanne Toussaint, introduced a whole series of enamelled-gold panther pieces, which proved to be very influential in this post-war period. By 1973, after the Cartier family had sold the business, a diffusion line was introduced to capture the lower-priced market. Mass-produced items, part of Le Must de Cartier, were sold through Must stores around the world. Articles including scarves, handbags and perfumes were added to the traditional gems.

Adolph Dassler

Adidas became a pioneer in developing specialised shoes for sports, and dominated the shoe industry until Nike surpassed it in the 1970s. It was one of the first pieces of apparel to establish a brand logo, in 1949, being made up of three stripes. It is a major sports apparel manufacturer, the group now including Reebok, Taylormade golf company and Rockport.

Born 1900, Herzogenaurach, Germany
Importance Pioneer in sports shoe industry
Died 1978, Herzogenaurach, Germany

The German shoe company was formed in 1920, when Adolph Dassler began a business that specialised in manufacturing slippers. Four years later his brother, Rudolph, joined him and the company began to produce football boots and track shoes. Their reputation grew when, during the 1936 Berlin Olympic Games, Jesse Owens won four gold medals wearing their shoes. After a rift in 1948, the brothers split and Rudolph founded Puma and Adolph formed Adidas.

The Adidas brand has long been popularised by sports stars, including Mohammed Ali, Martina Navratilova, Kobe Byrant and David Beckham. During the early 1980s, Adidas became very popular with hip-hop musicians and rap dancers. A song entitled *My Adidas* was recorded in which young African-American rappers immortalised the brand. Black urban youth, in particular,

'Impossible is nothing'

Adidas slogan

cultivated a cult association with the sports shoes and this new wave influenced youth worldwide. Adidas became an A-list brand that remains a popular cultural icon in today's society.

In these postmodern times, lifestyle and self-identity are often based on the type of popular cultural products that we consume and wear on a day-to-day basis. Like the T-shirt, sports shoes are a form of popular cultural attire. They break gender boundaries, as they appeal to both sexes, can be worn with almost anything and do not need to be colour coordinated.

In 2004, Stella McCartney, a top English fashion designer, launched a joint venture line with Adidas, establishing a long-term relationship with the firm. Similarly, Yohji Yamamoto was asked by Adidas if he would be interested in designing shoes for the company for sale in Japan and America. He agreed and has also committed to a number of projects for the future. The relationship inspired Yamamoto to become interested in sportswear in general and he has since opened a number of his own sportswear clothing shops in England.

Following its acquisition of Reebok in 2006, Adidas business sales drew closer to those of its major rival, Nike, in North America. In the same year, the company signed an 11-year deal to become the official National Basketball Association (NBA) apparel provider for basketball jerseys and 'Superstar' basketball shoes. For the 2008 Summer Olympics in Beijing, China, Adidas spent 70 million euros sponsoring the event.

Jean-Louis Dumas-Hermès

The 'Kelly' bag, one of the most coveted handbags in the world today, was fashioned by Hermès in the 1930s and named, in 1956, after the beautiful Hollywood actress, and Princess of Monaco, Grace Kelly. Hermès is a French high-fashion house specialising in leather, ready-to-wear lifestyle accessories and perfumery luxury goods. With an emphasis on quality, in both materials and workmanship for well over a century, the label has a long-standing reputation for luxury, status and good taste.

Born 1938, Paris, France
Importance
Producer of high-quality leather accessories

Hermès, a legendary family name in fine leather products, spans five generations. While today, the business is overseen by Jean-Louis Dumas-Hermès, the original 1837 business was founded by Thierry and his son Emile-Charles and catered for the wealthy carriage trade by making beautifully handcrafted harnesses and saddles. The third-generation owner, Emile-Maurice, catered for the automobile trade after the turn of the twentieth century by making car and fashion accessories such as belts, luggage, silk scarves and silver jewellery.

In 1837, the Hermès *carré*, or scarf, was introduced and a dedicated scarf factory was established in Lyon. Hermès purchased raw Chinese silk, spun it into yarn and wove it into a fabric twice as heavy and strong as most scarves on the market. Each was individually screen-printed with vegetable dye, each colour being left for a month to dry. Designers could choose from over 200,000 colours. Over the years, as natural materials became increasingly hard to find, Hermès struggled to compete with rival firms who used cheaper man-made products.

As well as their famous silk scarves, a number of other staple luxury items have become part of Hermès' classic collection, including the *chaine d'ancre* bracelet and the riding jacket outfit of 1937, men's silk ties in 1946 and the first perfume 'Eau d'Hermès' in 1949 followed by 'Caleche' in 1961. By the 1960s, the company had permanently entered the American market by offering its silk ties to the exclusive Newman Marcus department stores, and by the 1970s Hermès had outlets across Europe and Japan.

New designers, Eric Bergère and Bernard Sanz revamped the apparel collection in the1970s by adding python motorcycle jackets and ostrich-skin jeans, with Veronique Nichanian appointed as head designer since 1988. Their earliest men's leather jackets in the 1920s featured the first zips ever to be used in France, and were so unique that the Prince of Wales bought a zipped golfing jacket. For men, the Hermès signature line now includes leather jackets with Sherpa lining and trim, gabardine blazers and greatcoats and richly patterned ties. In 1998, they started their first womenswear department and hired the famous Belgian, Martin Margiela, to head the team. Originally an assistant to Jean-Paul Gaultier, Margiela was considered very avant-garde and his love of deconstruction made him the ideal designer to modernise the Hermès brand and attract a younger clientele.

Hermès is one of the few companies to have rejected signing licensing agreements for other businesses to manufacture goods bearing their label. This, of course, protects their reputation, and maintains close quality-control methods in their production and manufacturing. Although Hermès became a public company in 1993, the family retained an 80 per cent controlling share. The label now has expanded to include fine watches, perfumes and hand-painted porcelain.

HOLLYWOOD

Hollywood films were instrumental in spreading the influence of American popular culture around the world, and this included the fashion trends on the silver screen. Young and old, alike, copied the 'look' of the megastars – their make-up and hairstyles, in particular, but also accessories such as hats and jewellery, which were immediately mass-produced to make them affordable for mass consumption.

Hollywod had an influence on many areas of fashion. In the 1920s, Greta Garbo was renowned for wearing her cloche hat pulled down so far that the brim hid her eyebrows, inspiring a craze for cloche hats across the fashion industry. Platinum blondes dominated the 1930s sex-siren era. Hollywood designers, such as Gilbert Adrian, Howard Greer, Walter Plunkett and Edith Head, also worked for the wholesale trade in America, some of them emerging initially from New York's Seventh Avenue, the heart of the ready-to-wear garment industry.

Adrian, who was responsible for creating the enduring 1930s silver-screen look, designed his most successful commercial garment – a white organdie evening dress with ruffled shoulders – for Joan Crawford in the 1932 film *Letty Linton*. Following the release of the film, the dress sold 500,000 copies in Macy's New York department store. Similarly, Plunkett was immortalised for his costume design for Scarlett O'Hara in *Gone With the Wind* (1939). In the 1943 film *Stormy Weather*, Cab Calloway appeared dressed in an immaculate yet outrageously styled all-white suit, feathered fedora and white shoes, inspiring Afro-Americans to wear the oversized zoot suit as a badge of identity. Edith Head's most successful design was the dress she created for Elizabeth Taylor in the film *A Place in the Sun* (1951), which was reproduced and sold under her own label in department stores across

America. Westerns dominated the 1950s and the Stetson hats, boots, embroidered shirts and jackets and bootlace ties became the street style of the decade; street style has regularly been modelled on fashion portrayed in popular films.

The influence of Hollywood was not limited to the rag trade. International designers, like England's Mary Quant, included western-style woman's outfits in her first couture collection in 1961, and Yves Saint Laurent brought out Russian Cossack hats and coats with Persian lamb trim following the launch of the historical post-revolutionary film *Dr Zhivago* in 1965. He revisited the Russian theme with his 'Catherine the Great' collection of 1976. When Ralph Lauren designed the costumes for Woody Allen's 1978 film, *Annie Hall*, he influenced the way millions of women dressed at the time. In the film, Annie wore 1940s masculine clothes complete with waistcoats, ties, flat shoes and oversized trousers. The 1970s was the decade for classic revivalist films which brought back nostalgia for earlier times, including the 1940s. In turn, this interest saw the rise of the second-hand clothing businesses that proliferated for a number of decades.

Music associated with popular films also had an impact on trends. The Beatles, the Rolling Stones, Bob Dylan and others epitomised anti-fashion trends with their unconventional hairstyles, clothing and mixture of colours. Johnny Rotten and the Sex Pistols inspired even more polarised fashion trends, their music and appearance symbolizing anti-establishment sentiments. These rock band and musical personalities were often referenced in post-1960s Hollywood films and, in recent times, have become the central theme of many documentary film productions.

Manolo Blahnik

Manolo Blahnik is possibly the most famous shoe designer in the world. His shoes are fashion icons and are said to be objects not of desire, but of worship. They are ubiquitous at any red carpet event and worn by the world's best-dressed women.

Born 1942, Santa Cruz, Canary Islands
Importance Creates highly sought-after shoes that exude femininity, glamour and status

Blahnik studied international law, and then turned to architecture and literature, intending to become a set designer, before turning his attention to designing shoes. In the mid 1970s, he began designing footwear for English fashion designer Ossie Clark, who was looking for shoes that were innovative, futuristic and colourful, and for the Italian brand Fiorucci, Milan's hottest avant-garde designer label. He designed colourful, plastic sandals for Fiorucci called 'jellies', which sold worldwide. When Blahnik opened his first shop 'Zapata', just off the Kings Road in London, it instantly became popular among fashionable Londoners looking for sexy, sometimes witty creations. In the 1980s, Blahnik concentrated on making more elegant and sophisticated footwear. His shoes became known for their femininity, exquisite craftsmanship, and lightness of weight and construction. They were also admired for their vivid colour and fabric combinations.

Blahnik produces his shoes in small batches to maintain their exclusivity. Each pair goes through a process of 50 stages before it is hand-finished in his workshop in Italy. He becomes personally involved in the production and it is his attention to detail that makes his shoes so recognisable. He is fascinated with different textures, including brocade, satin and lace, and with trimmings such as fur-edging, jewelled highlights and ribbon ties. His designs are complex, eccentric and fantastical. They are often built around vertiginously high thin heels (Blahnik became famous for inventing the term 'toe cleavage'). Yet his inspirations came from classical design and the work of Madeleine Vionnet, Salvatore Ferragamo and Roger Vivier.

'People walk differently in high heels… Shall I call it suggestive? Shall I call it sensuous? You walk in a sensuous way. Your body sways to a different kind of tempo.'

Blahnik has worked with numerous top designers including John Galliano, Yves Saint Laurent, Bill Blass and Emanuel Ungaro who commissioned him to design shoes for their runway shows. When his shoes started appearing regularly in the hit television series *Sex in the City*, he became an international star in his own right. He designed a special pair of shoes for the star, Sarah Jessica Parker, called the 'SJP'. Owing to his international reputation and the attention that he has brought to British shoe design, Blahnik was awarded an OBE in 2007 for his services to British fashion.

Philip Treacy

Philip Treacy's hats are known for their mastery of skill, eccentricity, idiosyncrasy, fantasy and use of non-traditional millinery materials, including crystal and ram's horns. His hats are unique, one-of-a-kind creations, in the true sense of haute couture.

Born 1967, County Galway, Ireland
Importance Makes exquisite, one-of-a-kind headgear

Treacy began his studies at the National College of Art and Design, Dublin, in 1985, where he made hats as a hobby. In 1988, he enrolled in a master's degree course in fashion at the Royal College of Art, London, and the following year showed one of his hats to Michael Roberts, fashion editor of *Tatler* magazine, and Roberts' style editor, Isabella Blow. Immediately, Isabella Blow commissioned him to create a hat for her wedding. She went on to become his muse and a great champion of his work. He designed a number of extraordinary hats for her, looking more like sculpture than millinery.

Treacy's inspiration stretches from the surreal to the sculptural, and he enjoys the physicality of making something from nothing. According to Blow, Treacy was fascinated by birds, and he captured the concept of flight effectively in many of his creations, including his 'Feather-bone Dandelion' of 1992, made from cockerel feathers. Growing up in a tiny village on the west coast of Ireland, he made hats for his sister's dolls from the feathers shed by his mother's

'I make hats because I love hats. It's an enigmatic object that serves the human purpose only of beautification and embellishment and making one feel good whether you're the observer of the spectacle or the wearer.'

poultry: 'I love feathers. They're the most incredible material'.

Isabella Blow, a great benefactor of the fashion world, invited Treacy to set up a work-shop in her Belgravia home in 1990. The following year, he was commissioned by Karl Lagerfeld to make hats for Chanel Haute Couture Collections. Since then he has worked with many designers, including Alexander McQueen, Versace, Givenchy, Valentino and Ralph Lauren.

Treacy's collections of hats present strange silhouettes, architectural forms, lace and feather creations. One of his most publicised creations depicts a frigate called 'The Ship' – a replica of a French, eighteenth-century ship, with full rigging, made from millinery materials including miniature buttons. It was inspired when Treacy read about life in France during the 1750s, when ships featured in women's hairstyles when going to the opera, in celebration of naval military victory. Such women were applauded for supporting the French cause by wearing these headpieces.

Treacy's hats featured in the 1996 Florence Biennale and he collaborated with artist Vanessa Beecroft on an installation at the Venice Biennale in 2001. He has been awarded Britain's Designer of the Year award five times and gained an OBE in 2007, for his outstanding services to the British fashion industry.

Dare Jennings

Australian Dare Jennings launched the Mambo clothing label in 1984 as a surf and streetwear brand that appealed to the young and daring. It offered a stylish range of board shorts, T-shirts, skirts and swimwear for all members of the family. The label's unique artwork reflected the Australian love of nonconformity and featured 'the tooting dog' motif that has become an idiosyncratic Australian icon. This form of self-reflective humour is typically postmodern, and typically Australian.

Born 1950, New South Wales, Australia
Importance Raised status of Australian fashion with controversial designs

The business, which has grown from a backyard T-shirt screen-printing business into a multi-million dollar surf-wear company, was started in Australia by a group of young people producing graphic designs that were politically or religiously motivated, or humorous. While its mainstay was clothing, the brand also manufactured a range of other products as well, from watches to ceramics. Jennings commissioned a variety of artists to create images that were reproduced on Mambo fabrics. Artists included Gerry Wedd, a maker of ceramics and jewellery; Reg Mombassa (formerly Chris O'Doherty), a pop star from the band *Mental as Anything*; and a cartoonist, Matthew Martin. Their art and designs featured surreal suburban landscapes populated by vomiting dogs, horned bulls, boxy fibro houses and polluting smoke pouring from factory chimneys. These images presented a social critique relating to the perceived lack of humanity in the urban environment.

Jennings found that, prior to Mambo, most T-shirts and surf-wear decoration was copied from American brands and he realised the commercial power of provocative art and graphics. He admitted that his intentions were simply that he liked being controversial, breaking all expectations of stereotypical Australian surf-wear brands and portraying a different face of Australia to the world, one that was not based on the sun, sea and sand construction. As the youth market was the main target group of their brand – a sector immersed in popular cultural media such as cartoons and comics – Jennings appreciated that a mixture of brightly-coloured images, memorable patterns and text was important. He allowed artists enough artistic licence to create unique and individualised designs, and the constantly changing styles made the label difficult to copy. While this made the Mambo label unique, as it enticed buyers to engage with the ever-changing stylistic trademark, it also challenged accepted marketing ploys. Jennings rejected 'branding' protocols, such as a consistent logo or identity style, by continuing to adopt new styles with a seemingly endless supply of powerful ideas from his designers.

While the brand is about selling a lifestyle, it is also part of the anti-fashion statement where 'going against the status quo' makes people think. Mambo consistently challenges the accepted ideas of 'good taste' and ridicules popular Australian art beliefs and values. The brand has often been criticised for overstepping boundaries and protocols by using artwork that has been considered blasphemous and distinctly offensive. Despite this, the Australian Olympic team wore printed Hawaiian Mambo shirts for the 2000 Olympic ceremonies.

The company was sold in 2000 to the Gazal Corporation, a Sydney-based clothing manufacturer, which had distributed clothes for Mambo since 1990. With manufacturing carried out in various locations offshore, the labels now read 'made near Australia'.

Index

For main entries see contents page. References to fashion designers are given only where mentioned other than their main entry.